Crochet
BAKERY

WHO CAN RESIST MAKING YUMMY TREATS?

CAROLINE TURNER

TUVA

Tuva Publishing

www.tuvapublishing.com

Address Merkez Mah. Cavusbasi Cad. No:71
Cekmekoy - Istanbul 34782 / Turkey
Tel: +9 0216 642 62 62

Crochet Bakery

First Print 2021 / April

All Global Copyrights Belong To
Tuva Tekstil ve Yayıncılık Ltd.

Content Crochet
Editor in Chief Ayhan DEMİRPEHLİVAN
Project Editor Kader DEMİRPEHLİVAN
Designer Caroline TURNER
Technical Editors Wendi CUSINS, Leyla ARAS, Büşra ESER
Graphic Designers Ömer ALP, Abdullah BAYRAKÇI, Tarık TOKGÖZ
Cover Illustration Murat TANHU YILMAZ
Photograph Tuva Publishing

ISBN 978-605-7834-04-1

f TuvaYayincilik **p** TuvaPublishing
t TuvaYayincilik **o** TuvaPublishing

This book is dedicated to my Dad. You were here when I wrote it Dad, but you never got to see the completed book. I'm sure you would have been proud of the accomplishment. I will miss you and love you forever.

Thank you to my wonderful husband, son and family for your support during writing this book and putting up with yarn and design work everywhere! Thank you to my friend Sarah who encouraged me to try crochet and who has supported and helped me along the way (in more ways than one!). Thank you to Wendi, the wonderful technical editor, you have been invaluable!

Thank you to my publisher for your expert support and guidance along the way and giving me the opportunity to fulfil my ambition of writing a book. It's been a truly enjoyable, wonderful and delicious crochet journey!

CONTENTS

PROJECTS

INTRODUCTION

I am found of everything arts and crafts. I love painting in mixed media as well as crocheting. I've tried most crafts but crochet and painting are definitely my favorite.

I love creating personalities through my crochet and art. I'm very inspired by old stories and book excerpts. Creating a childlike pretend world is my aim.

The idea came about for this book when I bought dollhouse number four, an amazing dollhouse bakery which came with a variety of miniature cakes and I started making some miniature cakes myself using crochet and so the idea developed. I had great fun collecting inspirational images of cakes and pies, it certainly made me very hungry!

The dollhouse baker has made some great bakes - they could be ready to move into your own dollhouse in a flash as they are super quick to hook up.

They are cute little ornaments to have around the home. Why not make all the designs and set up your own Crochet Bakery?! Children will love them! Additionally, the cakes make great pin cushions and crochet accessory holders.

If you are new to crochet, there are lots of easy designs for you to try. You'll soon catch the crochet bug and want to create more.

As crochet is known for its relaxing therapeutic qualities, you are sure to get a sense of achievement and well-being, all at the same time.

I have a corner in my lounge I call "my crochet corner" where all my designs develop. It's a very messy, but it's my favourite corner in the world!

Writing a book and inspiring others has been an ambition, so by buying my book and making some of my patterns you are making my dream come true!

Beautiful Wedding Cake · Page 16

Bunny Cupcake · Page 22

Battenberg Cake Slice · Page 12

Carrot Cake Slice · Page 26

Cherry Slice and Ice Cream · Page 30

Chocolate & Strawberry Sponge Cake · Page 34

Fondant Fancies · Page 38

Fruit Donuts · Page 42

Giant Lollipops · Page 46

Happy Donuts · Page 52

Key Lime Pie · Page 56

Lemon Sponge Cake · Page 60

Mr. Ginger The Gingerbread Cookie · Page 64

Pink Swrill Cupcake · Page 68

Rainbow Cake · Page 72

Rose Cupcake · Page 78

Strawberry and Kiwi Fruit Dessert · Page 82

Jelly Rolls · Page 86

Wedding Cake Hanging Charm · Page 90

Dollhouse Penny Baker · Page 94

Materials Used in this Book

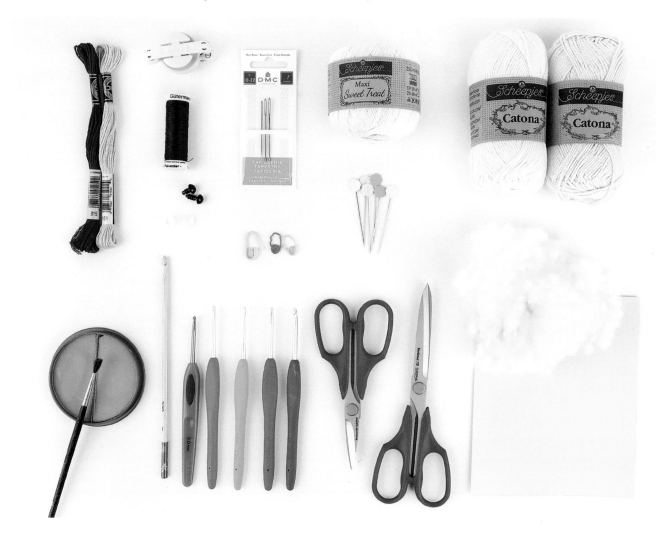

Yarns

I have used three Scheepjes weights of cotton yarn for the projects in this book.

- Scheepjes Catona
- Scheepjes Cahlista
- Scheepjes Maxi Sweet Treat

Scheepjes yarns come in many shades with recognizable shade numbers, to enable projects with a combination of yarn weights but using the same shades.

By using a different yarn weight you can make the project a different size. Make a bigger project by using thicker yarn than the pattern states and of course a suitable hook size increase will also be needed. Make a project smaller by using thinner yarn than the pattern states and of course a suitable hook size decrease will also be needed.

Yarn Weight Symbol & Category Names	0 LACE	1 SUPER FINE	2 FINE	3 LIGHT	4 MEDIUM	5 BULKY	6 SUPER BULKY	7 JUMBO
Type of Yarns in Category	Fingering 10-count crochet thread	Sock, Fingering Baby	Sport Baby	DK Light Worsted	Worsted Afghan, Aran	Chunky, Craft, Rug	Super Bulky, Roving	Jumbo Roving
Crochet Gauge Ranger in Single Crochet to 4 inch	32-42 double crochets**	21-32 sts	16-20 sts	12-17 sts	11-14 sts	8-11 sts	7-9 sts	6 sts and fewer
Recommended Hook in Metric Size Range	Steel*** 1.6-1.4mm Regular hook 2.25mm	2.25-3.5 mm	3.5-4.5 mm	4.5-5.5 mm	5.5-6.5 mm	6.5-9 mm	9-15 mm	15mm and larger
Recommended Hook U.S. Size Range	Steel*** 6,7,8 Regular hook B-1	B-1 to E-4	E-4 to 7	7 to 1-9	1-9 to K-10 1/2	K-10 1/2 to M-13	M-13 to Q	Q and larger

Catona

100% mercerised cotton fingering weight yarn comes in an enormous number of colours.
I have not used all of the shades but here are the magnificent range of shades available.

CATONA 50G

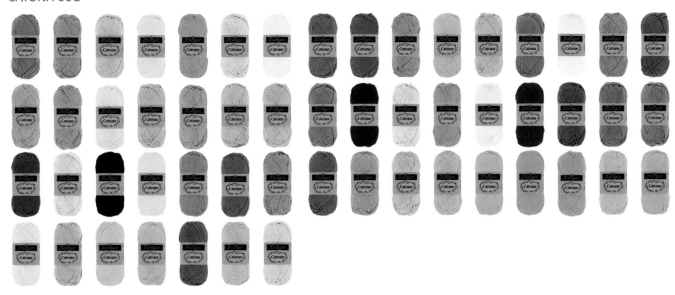

Cahlista

Cahlista means "beautiful one" and Cahlista definitely is! This 100% un-mercerized cotton Aran weight yarn has an optimised twist to reduce splitting whilst maintaining a soft drape. This yarn is double gassed, this means it is passed over a naked flame to singe away any random fibres, not once, but twice... creating a super smooth yarn that glides on the hook. Cahlista comes in 99 shades which match with the Catona range.

CAHLISTA 25G

Maxi Sweet Treat

Scheepjes Maxi Sweet Treat 25 grams is beautiful high twist mercerised cotton lace weight thread and is available in 87 shades. The colors match perfectly with the Catona yarns to enable you to mix and match. I used this yarn for some of the dollhouse bakery projects.

MAXI SWEET TREAT 25G

Mixed Media Ideas

Crochet always looks great but coming from a mixed media background, I would always say "Don't be afraid to experiment"! Have fun with added extras as well. Of course, you can always experiment with your own color choices for projects but here are some ideas that could help you further individualise your projects. Although, for safety reasons not all the ideas are suitable if you are giving the project to a child.

⚙ You can sew on shaped appliqué patches in felt or printed fabrics.

⚙ Paint designs onto your crochet (you can see an example of paint being used on the plate project in the Dollhouse Bakery pattern).

⚙ Glue patterned paper shapes onto your crochet.

⚙ Cut out images from wrapping papers or magazines and glue them on your project.

⚙ Embroider or cross stitch designs on top of the crochet. Single crochet lends itself to cross stitch as you can use the holes for cross stitches.

⚙ Add some sparkle with glued on glitter or sequins or even use sparkly yarns in place of the suggested yarns.

⚙ Add amigurumi faces with safety eyes and embroidered features.

⚙ Sew on different colored buttons.

⚙ Sew on ribbon/s.

⚙ Add some text by printing some text or using some text from a newspaper or magazine and gluing it on.

⚙ Add a homemade label and stick it onto a cocktail stick and stick this into the crochet project.

⚙ The rest is up to your imagination...... and HAVE FUN!

Battenberg
CAKE SLICE

Who can resist a slice of pink and yellow cake?

Materials

YARN

Scheepjes Catona 50g
- Color A: Soft Rose (409) – 1 ball
- Color B: Lemonade (403) – 1 ball
- Color C: English Tea (404) – 1 ball

PLUS

- Size D-3 (3.25mm) crochet hook (or suitable size for yarn used)
- Yarn needle
- Stitch marker/s
- Toy stuffing
- Card - Cut to about $3\frac{1}{8}$" (8 cm) square. (Optional)

FINISHED SIZE

- About $3\frac{1}{2}$" (9 cm) square

Pattern Notes

Four small squares are sewn together and then crocheted around. Two pieces are then joined together around a piece of card – to keep the shape.

(Note: If this project is intended for children, or if more than a sponge wipe will be needed for cleaning, then do not use the card insert.)

Assembled squares showing the two pieces of four squares each

Small Square (Make 8 - 4 using Color A & 4 using Color B)

Row 1: (Right Side) Ch 7, sc in 2nd ch from hook, sc in each each of next 5 ch. (6 sc)

Rows 2–6: Ch 1, turn, sc in each st across. (6 sc)

At the end of Row 6, fasten off, leaving a long tail for sewing.

Assembly

Using long tails and yarn needle, sew squares together alternating colors, to create two pieces of four squares each. Weave in all ends.

Edging (First piece)

Rnd 1: With right side facing, using Color C, join in any corner st on one assembled piece, ch 1, 3 sc in same corner st, *sc in each of next 10 sts, 3 sc in next corner st; repeat from * twice more, sc in each of next 10 sts; join with sl st to first sc. (52 sc).

Rnd 2: Ch 1, sc in each st around; join with sl st to first sc. (52 sc) Fasten off Color C and weave in all ends.

Rnd 3: With right side facing, using Color B, join in any corner st, ch 1, 3 sc in same corner st, *sc in each of next 12 sts, 3 sc in next corner st; repeat from * twice more, sc in each of next 12 sts; join with sl st to first sc. (60 sc)

Rnd 4: Ch 1, working in **back loops** only, sc in each sc around; join with sl st to first sc. (60 sc) Fasten off and weave in all ends.

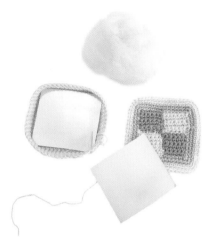

Inserting cards and stuffing

Edging (Second piece)

Rnds 1–4: Repeat Edging Rnds 1–4, but do not fasten off at the end of Round 4.

Rnds 5–7: Ch 1, sc in each st around. (60 sc)

At the end of Rnd 7, fasten off, leaving a long tail for sewing.

Aligning the pieces with card and stuffing inside

Finishing (Use photos as guide)

Cut two pieces of card to fit inside the pieces.

Insert one card in base of second piece (on wrong side) and stuff.

Insert the second card in base of first piece (on wrong side) and using long tail (from second piece) and yarn needle, sew the two pieces together, matching shaping and stitches (and making sure the colors align on either side).

Sewing around pieces, matching up corner stitches

Beautiful
WEDDING CAKE

Truly elegant and beautiful, the traditional
wedding cake design would be a wonderful
wedding present for a happy couple.

Materials

YARN	PLUS	FINISHED SIZE

Scheepjes Cahlista 50g
- Color A: Old Lace (130) – 6 ball

Scheepjes Catona 50g
- Color B: Scarlett (192) – 1 ball
- Color C: Old Rose (408) – 1 ball
- Color D: Lima (512) – 1 ball
- Color E: English Tea (404) – 1 ball

- Size # 7 (4.50mm) and size D-3 (3.25mm) crochet hook (or suitable size for yarn used)
- Yarn needle
- Stitch marker/s
- Toy stuffing
- Card

- Diameter of Base Board-About 12¾" (32.5 cm)
  Height-About 11" (28cm) tall

Pattern Notes

The Cake Base and Tiers are crocheted in continuous rounds.

Each Tier is constructed separately and then stuffed and sewn together.

Special Stitch

Popcorn Stitch (pc): Work 3 double crochets in the stitch specified. Remove the hook from the loop. Insert hook in first double crochet made, place loop back on hook and pull through the stitch.

Wedding Cake
Cake Board Base

Rnd 1: (Right Side) Using Color A and larger hook, make a magic ring, 6 sc into ring. (6 sc). DO NOT JOIN. Mark end of round and move marker each round.
Rnd 2: 2 sc in each st around. (12 sc)
Rnd 3: [2 sc in next st, sc in next st] around. (18 sc)
Rnd 4: [2 sc in next st, sc in each of next 2 sts] around. (24 sc)
Rnd 5: [2 sc in next st, sc in each of next 3 sts] around. (30 sc)
Rnd 6: [2 sc in next st, sc in each of next 4 sts] around. (36 sc)
Rnd 7: [2 sc in next st, sc in each of next 5 sts] around. (42 sc)
Rnd 8: [2 sc in next st, sc in each of next 6 sts] around. (48 sc)
Rnd 9: [2 sc in next st, sc in each of next 7 sts] around. (54 sc)
Rnd 10: [2 sc in next st, sc in each of next 8 sts] around. (60 sc)
Rnd 11: [2 sc in next st, sc in each of next 9 sts] around. (66 sc)
Rnd 12: [2 sc in next st, sc in each of next 10 sts] around. (72 sc)
Rnd 13: [2 sc in next st, sc in each of next 11 sts] around. (78 sc)
Rnd 14: [2 sc in next st, sc in each of next 12 sts] around. (84 sc)
Rnd 15: [2 sc in next st, sc in each of next 13 sts] around. (90 sc)
Rnd 16: [2 sc in next st, sc in each of next 14 sts] around. (96 sc)
Rnd 17: [2 sc in next st, sc in each of next 15 sts] around. (102 sc)
Rnd 18: [2 sc in next st, sc in each of next 16 sts] around. (108 sc)
Rnd 19: [2 sc in next st, sc in each of next 17 sts] around. (114 sc)
Rnd 20: [2 sc in next st, sc in each of next 18 sts] around. (120 sc)
Rnd 21: [2 sc in next st, sc in each of next 19 sts] around. (126 sc)
Rnd 22: [2 sc in next st, sc in each of next 20 sts] around. (132 sc)
Rnd 23: [2 sc in next st, sc in each of next 21 sts] around. (138 sc)
Rnd 24: [2 sc in next st, sc in each of next 22 sts] around. (144 sc)
Rnd 25: [2 sc in next st, sc in each of next 23 sts] around. (150 sc)
Rnd 26: Sc in each of next 12 sts, [2 sc in next st, sc in each of next 24 sts] 5 times, 2 sc in next st, sc in each of next 12 sts. (156 sc)
Rnd 27: Sc in each of next 13 sts, [2 sc in next st, sc in each of next 25 sts] 5 times, 2 sc in next st, sc in each of next 12 sts. (162 sc)
Rnd 28: Sc in each of next 6 sts, [2 sc in next st, sc in each of next 26 sts] 5 times, 2 sc in next st, sc in each of next 20 sts, sl st in next st. (168 sc)
Fasten off and weave in ends.

Bottom Tier

Rnds 1–21: Repeat Rounds 1 to 21 of Cake Board Base.
At the end of Round 21, there are 126 sc.
Rnd 22: Working in **back loops** only, sc in each st around. (126 sc)
Rnds 23–31: Sc in each st around. (126 sc)
Rnd 32: [pc in next st, sc in next st] around. (63 popcorns, 63 sc)
Fasten off, leaving a long tail for sewing.

Round 22 - Working in back loops only.

Middle Tier

Rnds 1–14: Repeat Rounds 1 to 14 of Cake Board Base.
At the end of Round 14, there are 84 sc.
Rnd 15: Working in **back loops** only, sc in each st around. (84 sc)
Rnds 16–24: Sc in each st around. (84 sc)
Rnd 25: [pc in next st, sc in next st] around.
(42 popcorns, 42 sc)
Fasten off, leaving a long tail for sewing.

Top Tier

Rnds 1–8: Repeat Rounds 1 to 8 of Cake Board Base.
At the end of Round 8, there are 48 sc.
Rnd 9: Working in **back loops** only, sc in each st around. (48 sc)
Rnds 10–18: Sc in each st around. (48 sc)
Rnd 19: [pc in next st, sc in next st] around.
(24 popcorns, 24 sc)
Fasten off, leaving a long tail for sewing.

CAKE DECORATIONS

Top Tier Lace Frosting

Row 1: (Right Side) Using Color E and smaller hook, ch 72, sc in 2nd ch from hook, sc in next ch, [ch 5, skip next 2 ch, sc in each of next 3 ch] 13 times, ch 5, skip next 2 ch, sc in each of last 2 ch.

Row 2: Ch 1, turn, sc in first st, [ch 8, sc in center sc of next 3-sc group] across, ending with ch 8, sc in last st. Fasten off, leaving a very long tail for sewing.

Middle Tier Lace Frosting

Row 1: (Right Side) Using Color E and smaller hook, ch 122, sc in 2nd ch from hook, sc in next ch, [ch 5, skip next 2 ch, sc in each of next 3 ch] 23 times, ch 5, skip next 2 ch, sc in each of last 2 ch.

Row 2: Repeat Row 2 of Top Tier Lace Frosting.

Bottom Tier Lace Frosting

Row 1: (Right Side) Using Color E and smaller hook, ch 172, sc in 2nd ch from hook, sc in next ch, [ch 5, skip next 2 ch, sc in each of next 3 ch] 33 times, ch 5, skip next 2 ch, sc in each of last 2 ch.

Row 2: Repeat Row 2 of Top Tier Lace Frosting.

The three completed Lace Frosting decorations.

Floral Base

Rnd 1: (Right Side) Using Color A and larger hook, make a magic ring, 6 sc into ring. (6 sc)

Rnd 2: 2 sc in each st around. (12 sc)

Rnd 3: [2 sc in next st, sc in next st] around. (18 sc)

Rnd 4: [2 sc in next st, sc in each of next 2 sts] around. (24 sc)

Rnds 5–7: Sc in each st around. (24 sc)

At the end of Round 7, sl st in next st and fasten off, leaving a tail for sewing.

Rose (make 16 - 8 each of Color B & Color C)

Rnd 1: (Right Side) Using smaller hook, ch 20, dc in 4th ch from hook (skipped chs count as first dc), [2 dc in next st, dc in each of next 3 sts] 4 times. (21 dc)

Fasten off, leaving a long tail for sewing.

Leaf (make 8)

Row 1: (Right Side) Using Color D and smaller hook, ch 7, sc in 2nd ch from hook, *hdc in next ch, dc in each of next 2 chs, hdc in next ch*, (sc, ch 2, sc) in last ch, working in unused lps on other side of starting ch, repeat from *to* once; ch 2; join with sl st to first sc. Fasten off, leaving a long tail for sewing.

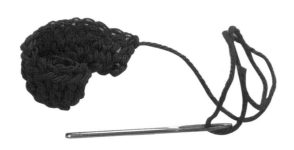

Completed leaf

○ Curl Rose and using yarn needle and long tail, stitch into shape.

Curled Rose getting sewn into shape.

Assembly

○ Cut out circles of card to fit into the base of each tier. Place them inside (making sure the wrong side is on the inside) and stuff the tiers.

Marking and cutting card to fit tiers

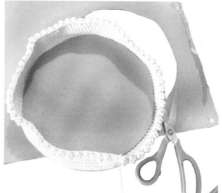

Card placed inside the base of tier

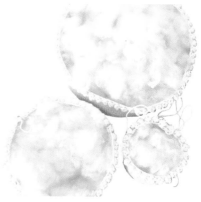

Three tiers stuffed and ready to sew

◉ Cut out large circle of card to fit Base Board and glue card to wrong side of Base Board.

◉ With right side of Base Board facing, flip the largest bottom tier (card base is at the top), and position and sew to the center of the Base Board.

◉ Similarly, sew the middle tier to center of bottom tier, and top tier to center of middle tier.

◉ Pin Roses and Leaves to right side of Floral Base and sew in place.

Sewing on Roses

Only two more leaves to sew in place

○○○○○○○○○○○○○○○○○○○○○○○

Finishing – use photos as a guide

◉ Pin Lace Frostings in position on the relevant tiers, lining up foundation chain to the unworked front loops. Match up the ends and sew in place.

Pinning Top Tier Lace Frosting in place

Match up the ends properly prior to sewing in place

◉ Stuff the Floral Base and position and sew to center of Top Tier.

Floral top decoration sewn on top of top tier

Bunny
CUPCAKE

Whip up a cute Bunny Cupcake for "somebunny" who
loves cupcakes! She is super quick to make - in fact,
She will hop right off your hook!

Materials

YARN

Scheepjes Catona 50g
- Main Color (MC): Garden Rose (251) – 1 ball (for Cupcake Case)
- Color A: Old Lace (130) – 1 ball
- Color B: Rich Coral (410) - small amount for Flower
- Color C: Lemon (280) - small amount for Flower

PLUS

- Size D-3 (3.25 mm) crochet hook (or suitable size for yarn used)
- Yarn needle
- Stitch marker/s
- Toy stuffing
- 2 x ¼" (6 mm) Safety Eyes
- Blusher and small brush (or cotton bud) for cheeks
- Pink embroidery floss or yarn for the ear and nose embroidery.

FINISHED SIZE

- About 3½" (9 cm wide, and 4¼" (11 cm) tall, including ears

Pattern Notes

The Topping is worked in continuous rounds, with the Ears, Tail and Flower worked separately and sewn on.

Cupcake Case

Using MC, make one complete Cupcake Case – page 112

Topping

Rnd 1: (Right Side) Using Color A, make a magic ring; 8 sc into the ring. (8 sc) DO NOT JOIN. Mark end of round and move marker each round.
Rnd 2: [2 sc in next st, sc in next st] around. (12 sc)
Rnd 3: Repeat Rnd 2. (18 sc)
Rnd 4: [2 sc in next st, sc in each of next 2 sts] around. (24 sc)
Rnd 5: Repeat Rnd 4. (32 sc)
Rnd 6: [2 sc in next st, sc in each of next 3 sts] around. (40 sc)
Rnds 7–12: Sc in each st around. (40 sc)
At the end of Round 12, fasten off, leaving a long tail for sewing.

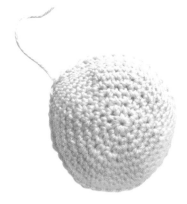

End of Rnd 12. Completed Cupcake Topping

Bunny Ear (Make 2)

Rnd 1: (Right Side) Using Color A, make a magic ring. 6 sc into the ring. (6 sc) DO NOT JOIN. Mark end of round and move marker each round.
Rnd 2: 2 sc in each st around. (12 sc)
Rnds 3–5: Sc in each st around. (12 sc)
Rnd 6: [sc in next st, sc2tog] around. (8sc)
Rnds 7–9: Sc in each st around. (8 sc)
At the end of Round 9, fasten off leaving tail for sewing.

Lightly stuff the Ears.

End of Rnd 9 – Both Bunny Ears completed.

Bunny Tail

Using Color A, make a small pom-pom. Brush the yarn to give it some more fluffiness. Trim to uniform sphere shape if required.

Trimming brushed pom-pom into shape

Flower

Rnd 1: Using Color B, make a magic ring, 6 sc into ring; join with sl st to first sc. (6 sc)
Rnd 2: [Ch 3, sl st in next st] 6 times. (6 ch-3 loops)
Fasten off, leaving a tail for sewing.

Using Color C, embroider 3 French Knots in the center of Flower.

End of Flower Round 2

Finishing - Use photos as a guide

⚙ Insert Safety Eyes in Cupcake Topping on Round 9, about 6 stitches apart.

⚙ Stuff Cupcake Case and Topping. Using long tails and yarn needle, sew the Topping to the inside stitches on Round 10 of Cupcake Case.

⚙ Using pink embroidery floss or yarn, embroider detail on each Ear using back stitches.
Position and pin Bunny Ears and Tail on cupcake and sew in place.

⚙ Apply blusher to add rosy cheeks.

⚙ Using the same floss or yarn as used on Ears, embroider Nose using satin stitch, to front of face.

⚙ Position Flower under one Ear and using long tail and yarn needle, sew in place.

Stuffing Cupcake Case and Topping

Cupcake Case and Topping sewn together

Embroidery detail on Ears

Back view of Bunny Tail

Carrot
CAKE SLICE

Is Carrot Cake the healthiest of all cakes?
Well this one certainly is.... No calories here!

Materials

YARN

Scheepjes Catona 50g
- Color A: Saffron (249) – 1 ball
- Color B: Old Lace (130) – 1 ball
- Color C: Sweet Orange (411) – small amount for Carrot
- Color D: Kiwi (205) – small amount for Carrot

PLUS

- Size D-3 (3.25 mm) crochet hook (or suitable size for yarn used)
- Yarn needle
- Stitch marker/s
- Toy stuffing

FINISHED SIZE

- About 4⅜" (11 cm) wide and 3⅛" (8 cm) long.

Pattern Notes

All the pieces for the Cake are worked in turned rows. The pieces are then sewn together and stuffed to form the cake slice.

Special Stitches

Popcorn Stitch (pc): Work 4 double crochets in the stitch specified. Remove the hook from the loop. Insert hook in first double crochet made, place loop back on hook and pull through the stitch. Ch 1 to secure.

⊙⊙⊙⊙⊙⊙⊙⊙⊙⊙⊙⊙⊙⊙⊙⊙⊙⊙⊙⊙⊙⊙⊙

Cake Slice

Creamy Topping

Row 1: (Right Side) Using Color B, ch 21, sc in 2nd ch from hook, pc in next ch, [sc in next ch, pc in next ch] 9 times. (10 popcorns, 10 sc)

Row 2: (Wrong Side) Ch 1, turn, sc in each st across. (20 sc)

Row 3: Ch 1, turn, [sc in next st, pc in next st] 10 times. (10 popcorns, 10 sc)

Fasten off, leaving a long tail for sewing.

Sides (Make 2)

Row 1: (Right Side) Using Color A, ch 21, sc in 2nd ch from hook, sc in each of next 19 ch. (20 sc)

Rows 2–6: Ch 1, turn, sc in each st across. (20 sc)
Change to Color B.

Rows 7–8: Ch 1, turn, sc in each st across. (20 sc)
Change to Color A.

Rows 9–14: Ch 1, turn, sc in each st across. (20 sc)
Change to Color B.

Row 15: Ch 1, turn, sc in each st across. (20 sc)

For the first Cake Side, fasten off and weave in ends. For the second Cake Side, fasten off, leaving a long tail for sewing.

Base

Row 1: (Right Side) Using Color A, ch 21, sc in 2nd ch from hook, sc in each of next 19 ch. (20 sc)

Rows 2–3: Ch 1, turn, sc in each st across. (20 sc)

Fasten off, leaving a long tail for sewing.

Ends (Make 2)

Row 1: (Right Side) Using Color A, ch 4, sc in 2nd ch from hook, sc in each of next 2 ch. (3 sc)

Rows 2–6: Ch 1, turn, sc in each st across. (3 sc)
Change to Color B.

Rows 7–8: Ch 1, turn, sc in each st across. (3 sc)
Change to Color A.

Rows 9–14: Ch 1, turn, sc in each st across. (3 sc)
Change to Color B.

Row 15: Ch 1, turn, sc in each st across. (3 sc)

Fasten off, leaving a long tail for sewing.

Cake Slice pieces ready to assemble

⊙⊙⊙⊙⊙⊙⊙⊙⊙⊙⊙⊙⊙⊙⊙⊙⊙⊙⊙⊙⊙⊙

Carrot

Rnd 1: (Right Side) Using Color C, make a magic ring, 4 sc into ring. (4 sc) DO NOT JOIN. Mark end of round and move marker each round.

Rnd 2: Sc in each st around. (4 sc)

Rnd 3: [2 sc in next st, sc in next st] twice. (6 sc)

Rnd 4: Sc in each st around. (6 sc)

Rnd 5: [2 sc in next st, sc in next st] 3 times. (9 sc)

Rnds 6–8: Sc in each st around. (9 sc)

At the end of Round 8, fasten off leaving a long tail.

Stuff Carrot lightly.
Using yarn needle, weave tail through the front loops of each of the 9 stitches on the last round, and pull closed. Thread through center of Carrot and secure.

Weaving the tail through the front loops

Carrot Top

Using Color D, [ch 4, sl st in 2nd ch from hook, sl st in each of next 2 chs] 5 times. (5 leaves) Fasten off leaving long tail.

Curl Carrot Top into shape and using long tail and yarn needle, sew to secure in shape.

Carrot Top showing the five leaves

Curled Carrot Top sewn into shape

Assembly

Sew Sides, Ends and Base of Cake Slice together with right sides on the outside. Stuff and sew on Topping, with right side on the outside.

Sew Carrot Top to top of Carrot.

Finishing

⬤ Sew Carrot to top of Cake Slice.

Completed Carrot Cake Slice

Top view

Cherry Slice and
ICE CREAM

One slice is never enough! Why not make several slices so the whole family gets a cherry treat?

Materials

YARN

Scheepjes Catona 50g
- Color A: Topaz (179) – 1 ball
- Color B: Rosewood (258) – 1 ball
- Color C: Primrose (522) – 1 ball

PLUS

- Yarn and materials for Cherries (page 110)
- Size D-3 (3.25 mm) crochet hook (or suitable size for yarn used)
- Yarn needle
- Stitch marker/s
- Toy stuffing

FINISHED SIZE

- Slice measures about 3⅔" (9.5 cm) wide (widest point); about 4¼" (10.8 cm) long; and about 2¼" (5.7 cm) high.
- Ice cream is about 2" (5 cm) diameter and about 2" (5 cm) high (excluding melted bits).

Pattern Notes

The pieces making up the Pie Slice are worked in back and forth rows.

The Ice Cream is worked in rounds.

When working the wrong side row after the Popcorn row, work in the top of the popcorn stitches.

Special Stitches

Popcorn Stitch (pc): Work 4 double crochets in the stitch specified. Remove the hook from the loop. Insert hook in first double crochet made, place loop back on hook and pull through the stitch. Ch 1 to secure.

Picot: Ch 3, sl st in first chain made.

◎◎◎◎◎◎◎◎◎◎◎◎◎◎◎◎◎◎◎◎◎◎◎

Cherry Pie Slice

Crust Base

Row 1: (Wrong Side) Using Color A, ch 3, sc in 2nd ch from hook, sc in last ch. (2 sc)

Row 2: Ch 1, turn, 2 sc in each st across. (4 sc)

Rows 3-4: Ch 1, turn, sc in each st across. (4 sc)

Row 5: Ch 1, turn, 2 sc in first st, [sc in next st] across to last st, 2 sc in last st. (6 sc)

Rows 6-7: Ch 1, turn, sc in each st across. (6 sc)

Rows 8-22: Repeat Rows 5-7 five times.

At the end of Row 22, there are 16 sc.

Row 23: Repeat Row 5 once more. (18 sc)

Row 24: Ch 1, turn, working in **back loops** only, sc in each st across. (18 sc)

Rows 25-32: Ch 1, turn, sc in each st across. (18 sc)

At the end of Row 32, fasten off and weave in ends.

Cherry Topping

Row 1: (Right Side) Using Color B, ch 3, sc in 2nd ch from hook, sc in last ch. (2 sc)

Row 2: Ch 1, turn, 2 sc in each st across. (4 sc)

Row 3: Ch 1, turn, sc in first st, pc in next st, sc in each of next 2 sts. (3 sc, 1 popcorn)

Row 4: Ch 1, turn, sc in each st across. (4 sc)

Row 5: Ch 1, turn, 2 sc in first st, [sc in next st] across to last st, 2 sc in last st. (6 sc)

Row 6: Ch 1, turn, sc in each st across. (6 sc)

Row 7: Ch 1, turn, sc in first st, [pc in next st, sc in next st] twice, pc in last st. (3 sc, 3 popcorns)

Row 8: Ch 1, turn, 2 sc in first st, [sc in next st] across to last st, 2 sc in last st. (8 sc)

Row 9: Ch 1, turn, sc in each of first 3 sts, pc in next st, sc in each of next 4 sts. (7 sc, 1 popcorn)

Row 10: Ch 1, turn, sc in each st across. (8 sc)

Row 11: Ch 1, turn, 2 sc in first st, pc in next st, sc in each of next 3 sts, pc in next st, sc in next st, 2 sc in last st. (8 sc, 2 popcorn)

Row 12: Ch 1, turn, sc in each st across. (10 sc)

Row 13: Ch 1, turn, sc in each of first 4 sts, pc in next st, sc in each of next 5 sts. (9 sc, 1 popcorn)

Row 14: Ch 1, turn, 2 sc in first st, [sc in next st] across to last st, 2 sc in last st. (12 sc)

Row 15: Ch 1, turn, sc in first st, pc in next st, sc in each of next 5 sts, pc in next st, sc in next st, pc in next st, sc in each of last 2 sts. (9 sc, 3 popcorns)

Row 16: Ch 1, turn, sc in each st across. (12 sc)

Row 17: Ch 1, turn, 2 sc in first st, sc in next st, pc in next st, sc in next st, pc in next st, sc in each of next 5 sts, 2 sc in last st. (12 sc, 2 popcorns)

Row 18: Ch 1, turn, sc in each st across. (14 sc)

Row 19: Ch 1, turn, pc in first st, sc in each of next 2 sts, pc in next st, sc in each of next 5 sts, pc in next st, sc in each of next 4 sts. (11 sc, 3 popcorns)

Row 20: 2 sc in first st, sc in each of next 12 sts, 2 sc in last st. (16 sc)

Fasten off, leaving a long tail for sewing.

Cherry Sides (make 2)

Row 1: (Right Side) Using Color B, ch 21, sc in 2nd ch from hook, sc in each of next 19 ch. (20 sc)

Rows 2-7: Ch 1, turn, sc in each st across. (20 sc)

At the end of Row 7, fasten off.

The Pie Slice pieces before assembly

Cherries

Make one complete Cherries – page 110

Ice Cream

Scoop of Ice Cream

Rnd 1: (Right Side) Using Color C, make a magic ring, 6 sc into ring. (6 sc) DO NOT JOIN. Mark end of round and move marker each round.

Rnd 2: 2 sc in each st around. (12 sc)

Rnd 3: [2 sc in next st, sc in next st] around. (18 sc)

Rnd 4: [2 sc in next st, sc in each of next 2 sts] around. (24 sc)

Rnd 5: [2 sc in next st, sc in each of next 3 sts] around. (30 sc)

Rnds 6–9: Sc in each st around. (30 sc)
Rnd 7: [Sc2tog in next st, sc in each of next 3 sts] around. (24 sc)
Rnd 8: [Sc2tog in next st, sc in each of next 2 sts] around. (18 sc)
Sl st in next st, and fasten off leaving a long tail for sewing.

Melted Ice Cream Base

Rnds 1–5: Repeat Rounds 1 to 5 of Scoop of Ice Cream.
At the end of Round 5, there are 30 sc.
Rnd 6: [2 hdc in next st, dc in each of next 4 sts, 2 hdc in next st, sc in each of next 4 sts] 3 times. (12 hdc, 12 dc, 12 sc)
Rnd 7: Ch 3, 2 tr in next st, picot, ch 3, sl st in each of next 3 sts, ch 6, sl st in 2nd ch from hook, sc in next ch, hdc in next ch, dc in each of next 2 ch, skip next 2 sts, sl st in next st.
Fasten off and weave in ends.

Round 7: Shows the skipped stitches before last slip stitch.

Finishing - Use photos as a guide

Sew the length of each Cherry Side to either side of Crust Base, starting from the point. Fold Crust Base along Row 24 and sew the edges of Cherry Sides up the Crust Base.
Stuff the pie.
Sew the Cherry Topping to Sides along the second last row of Crust.
Stuff the Scoop of Ice Cream and sew to Melted Ice Cream Base.
Sew Cherries on Ice Cream.
Optional: Sew Ice Cream to Cherry Pie

Chocolate & Strawberry
SPONGE CAKE

When you can't decide between chocolate or strawberry...

Make both! Extra cream, anyone?

Materials

YARN	PLUS	FINISHED SIZE
Scheepjes Catona 50g **For Chocolate Cake** ⬤ Color A: Chocolate (507) - 1 ball ⬤ Color B: Old Lace (130) - 1 ball **For Strawberry Cake** ⬤ Color A: Powder Pink (238) - 1 ball ⬤ Color B: Tropic (253) - 1 ball ⬤ Color C: Old Lace (130) – small amount for Cream	⬤ Yarn and materials for Cherries (page 110) and Strawberry (page 110) ⬤ Size D-3 (3.25mm) crochet hook (or suitable size for yarn used) ⬤ Yarn needle ⬤ Stitch marker/s ⬤ Toy stuffing	⬤ About 5" (12.5 cm) tall - including fruit topping.

Pattern Notes
⚙ The Main Cake and Frosting are worked in continuous rounds.
The pieces are then stuffed and sewn together, before adding the decorations.

⊙⊙⊙⊙⊙⊙⊙⊙⊙⊙⊙⊙⊙⊙⊙⊙⊙⊙⊙⊙⊙⊙⊙

Main Cake
Rnd 1: (Right Side) Using Color A, make a magic ring, 6 sc into ring. (6 sc) DO NOT JOIN. Mark end of round and move marker each round.
Rnd 2: 2 sc in each st around. (12 sc)
Rnd 3: [2 sc in next st, sc in next st] around. (18 sc)
Rnd 4: [2 sc in next st, sc in each of next 2 sts] around. (24 sc)
Rnd 5: [2 sc in next st, sc in each of next 3 sts] around. (30 sc)
Rnd 6: [2 sc in next st, sc in each of next 4 sts] around. (36 sc)
Rnd 7: Working in **back loops** only, sc in each st around. (36 sc)
Rnds 8–11: Sc in each st around. (36 sc)
Change to Color B.
Rnds 12–13: Sc in each st around. (36 sc)
Change to Color A.
Rnds 14–19: Sc in each st around. (36 sc)
At the end of Round 19, sl st in next st, and fasten off leaving long tail for sewing.

Top Frosting
Rnd 1: (Right Side) Using Color B, make magic ring, 6 sc into ring. (6 sc) DO NOT JOIN. Mark end of round and move marker each round.
Rnd 2: 2 sc in each st around. (12 sc)
Rnd 3: Working in **back loops** only, [2 sc in next st, sc in next st] around. (18 sc)
Rnd 4: Working in **back loops** only, [2 sc in next st, sc in each of next 2 sts] around. (24 sc)
Rnd 5: Working in **back loops** only, [2 sc in next st, sc in each of next 3 sts] around. (30 sc)
Rnd 6: Working in **back loops** only, [2 sc in next st, sc in each of next 4 sts] around. (36 sc)
Rnd 7: Working in **back loops** only, [2 sc in next st, sc in each of next 5 sts] around. (42 sc)

Rnd 8: Working in both loops, sc in each st around. (42 sc)
Rnd 9: [Sc2tog, sc in each of next 5 sts] around. (36 sc)
Sl st in next st, and fasten off leaving long tail for sewing.

Completed Main Cake and Top Frosting

Cherries (for Chocolate Cake)
Make one complete Cherries – page 110

Cream Topping (for Strawberry Cake)
Rnd 1: Using Color C, make a magic ring, 6 sc into ring. (6 sc) DO NOT JOIN. Mark end of round and move marker each round.
Rnd 2: 2 sc in each st around. (12 sc)
Rnd 3: Ch 2, 4 dc in each st around. (48 dc)
Sl st in next st, and fasten off leaving a tail for sewing.

Strawberry (for Strawberry Cake)
Make one complete Strawberry – page 110

⊙⊙⊙⊙⊙⊙⊙⊙⊙⊙⊙⊙⊙⊙⊙⊙⊙⊙⊙⊙⊙⊙⊙

Finishing - Use photos as a guide

Stuff Main Cake and Top Frosting and sew them together.

For Chocolate Cake:
Position and sew Cherries on top of the Cake.

For Strawberry Cake:
Position and sew Cream Topping and Strawberry on top of the Cake.

Completed Cake
with Top Frosting

Finished Chocolate Cake
with Cherries sewn on top.

Finished Strawberry Cake
with Cream & Strawberry.

Fondant
FANCIES

These yummy looking Fondant Fancies can also be used as a fun little holder for your crochet accessories!

Materials

YARN	PLUS	FINISHED SIZE

Scheepjes Catona 50g
- Color A: Lemonade (403) - 1 ball
- Color B: Powder Pink (238) - 1 ball
- Color C: Soft Rose (409) – 1 ball

- Size D-3 (3.25 mm) crochet hook (or suitable size for yarn used)
- Yarn needle
- Stitch marker/s
- Toy stuffing
- Embroidery floss or yarn in pink and white – for frosting "drizzles".

- Each Fondant Fancy is about 2" (5 cm) tall.

Pattern Notes

The Small Cake is worked from the top down, starting with joined rounds and then continuous rounds. The square Base and round Top are then sewn on after stuffing.

⊙⊙⊙⊙⊙⊙⊙⊙⊙⊙⊙⊙⊙⊙⊙⊙⊙⊙⊙⊙⊙⊙⊙⊙⊙

Fondant Fancy (make 6 – 2 in each color)

Small Cake

Rnd 1: (Right Side) Using chosen color, make a magic ring, 8 sc into ring; join with sl st to first sc.

Rnd 2: Ch 1, 2 sc in same st as joining, [2 sc in next st] around; join with sl st to first sc. (16 sc)

Rnd 3: Ch 3 (counts as first dc, now and throughout), 2 dc in first st (first corner made), hdc in next st, sc in next st, hdc in next st, [3 dc in next st (next corner made), hdc in next st, sc in next st, hdc in next st] 3 times; join with sl st to first dc (3rd ch of beg ch-3). (12 dc, 8 hdc, 4 sc)

Rnd 4: Ch 1, working in **back loops** only, sc in each st around. (24 sc) DO NOT JOIN. Mark end of round and move marker each round.

Rnds 5–9: Sc in each st all around. (24 sc)

At the end of Round 9, sl st in next st, and fasten off leaving long tail for sewing.

Stuff the small cake.

Round 3 – Making the corners

⊙⊙⊙⊙⊙⊙⊙⊙⊙⊙⊙⊙⊙⊙⊙⊙⊙⊙⊙⊙⊙⊙⊙⊙

Cake Base

Rnds 1–3: Using same Small Cake Color, repeat Rounds 1 to 3 of Small Cake.

At the end of Round 3, fasten off leaving a long tail for sewing.

Cake Topping

Rnd 1: (Right Side) Using same Small Cake Color, make a magic ring; 6 sc into ring. (6 sc) DO NOT JOIN. Mark end of round and move marker each round.

Rnd 2: 2 sc in each st around. (12 sc)

Rnd 3: Sc in each st around. (12 sc)

Sl st in next st, and fasten off leaving long tail for sewing.

Finished Cake Base

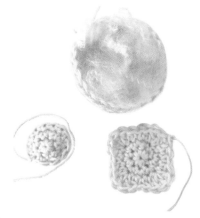

The completed cake pieces ready for sewing together

Finishing - Use photos as a guide

With right sides facing, sew the base onto the cake, matching
corner stitches. Add more stuffing if necessary.
Position and sew the lightly stuffed Cake Topping to top of
Small Cake.
Weave in all ends.
Embroider long stitches for frosting drizzles across top of
Cake and Topping.

Frosting drizzle detail

Fruit
DONUTS

Fruity-licious! Fruity zero calorie donut heaven.
Watermelon, Apple, Kiwi and Strawberry...
How refreshing!

Materials

YARN	PLUS	FINISHED SIZE

Scheepjes Catona 50g
- Main Color (MC): Topaz (179) – 1 ball
- Color A: English Tea (404)- 1 ball
- Color B: Cherry (413) - 1 ball
- Color C: Kiwi (205) – 1 ball

- Size #7 (4.50 mm) crochet hook (or suitable size for yarn used)
- Yarn needle
- Stitch marker/s
- Toy stuffing
- Embroidery floss or yarn in black and yellow – for seeds

- Each Donut is about 3½" (9 cm) diameter.

Pattern Notes

Each Donut consists of a base and a top, worked in continuous rounds, then sewn together. The tops are then decorated with embroidery stitches.

○○○○○○○○○○○○○○○○○○○○○○○

Donut Base (make 4 – 1 for each Donut)

Using MC:

Rnd 1: (Right Side) Make a magic ring; 6 sc into ring. (6 sc) DO NOT JOIN. Mark end of round and move marker each round.

Rnd 2: 2 sc in each st around. (12 sc)

Rnd 3: [2 sc in next st, sc in next st] around. (18 sc)

Rnd 4: [2 sc in next st, sc in each of next 2 sts] around. (24 sc)

Rnd 5: [2 sc in next st, sc in each of next 3 sts] around. (30 sc)

Rnd 6: [2 sc in next st, sc in each of next 4 sts] around. (36 sc)

Rnds 7–9: Sc in each st around. (36 sc)

At the end of Round 9, fasten off, leaving a long tail for sewing.

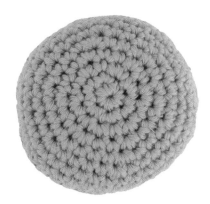

Completed Donut Base

○○○○○○○○○○○○○○○○○○○○○○○

Donut Top – Apple

Rnds 1–6: Using Color A, repeat Rounds 1 to 6 of Donut Base. At the end of Round 6, there are 36 sc.

Rnd 7: Sc in each st around. (36 sc)

Change to Color B.

Rnds 8–9: Sc in each st around. (36 sc)

At the end of Round 9, fasten off, leaving a long tail for sewing.

Apple Leaf (make 2)

Rnd 1: (Right Side) Using Color C, make a magic ring, [sc, 3 dc, 2 sc] into ring; close ring. (3 sc, 3 dc)

Fasten off leaving long tail for sewing.

Donut Top – Kiwi Fruit

Rnds 1–2: Using Color A, repeat Rounds 1 to 2 of Donut Base. At the end of Round 2, there are 12 sc.

Change to Color C.

Rnds 3–6: Repeat Rounds 3 to 6 of Donut Base. At the end of Round 6, there are 36 sc.

Rnds 7–9: Sc in each st around. (36 sc)

At the end of Round 9, fasten off, leaving a long tail for sewing.

Donut Top – Kiwi Fruit

Rnds 1–2: Using Color A, repeat Rounds 1 to 2 of Donut Base. At the end of Round 2, there are 12 sc.

Change to Color C.

Rnds 3–6: Repeat Rounds 3 to 6 of Donut Base. At the end of Round 6, there are 36 sc.

Rnds 7–9: Sc in each st around. (36 sc)

At the end of Round 9, fasten off, leaving a long tail for sewing.

Donut Top – Watermelon

Rnds 1–6: Using Color B, repeat Rounds 1 to 6 of Donut Base. At the end of Round 6, there are 36 sc.

Change to Color A.

Rnd 7: Sc in each st around. (36 sc)

Change to Color C.

Rnds 8–9: Sc in each st around. (36 sc)

At the end of Round 9, fasten off, leaving a long tail for sewing.

Donut Top – Strawberry

Rnds 1–9: Using Color B, repeat Rounds 1 to 9 of Donut Base. At the end of Round 9, there are 36 sc. Fasten off, leaving a long tail for sewing.

Strawberry Stalk

Rnd 1: (Right Side) Using Color C, make a magic ring, 6 sc into ring. (6 sc) DO NOT JOIN.

Rnd 2: [Sl st, ch 1, dc, ch 1] in each st around; join with sl st to first sl st. (6 sl st, 6 dc, 12 ch)

Fasten off, leaving a long tail for sewing.

Finishing - Use photos as a guide

Using yellow embroidery floss or yarn, embroider seeds on the right side of the Strawberry Donut Top.
Using black embroidery floss or yarn, embroider seeds on the rights sides of Kiwi Fruit, Apple and Watermelon Donut Tops.

With right sides facing, sew a Donut Base and Donut Top together, stuffing as you go.
Sew on Apple Leaves & Strawberry Stalk.
Weave in all ends.

Apple

Watermelon

Kiwi Fruit

Strawberry

Giant
LOLLIPOPS

Your teeth will not get any cavities with these Lollipops. But which one to choose..? The one with a Swirl or the Round one. Hmmm.. Perhaps I'll try both!

Materials

YARN

Scheepjes Catona 50g

Swirl Lollipop
- Color A: Cherry (413)- 1 ball
- Color B: Freesia (519) - 1 ball
- Color C: Old Rose (408) – 1 ball

Round Lollipop
- Color A: Tropic (253) – 3 balls

PLUS

For Swirl Lollipop
- Size #7 (4.50 mm) crochet hook (or suitable size for yarn used)
- Card (or craft foam)

For Round Lollipop
- Size K-10½ (6.50 mm) crochet hook (or suitable size for yarn used)

For Each Lollipop
- Yarn needle
- 3 x Stitch markers
- Toy stuffing
- Small amount of black embroidery floss or yarn – for mouth

- Large lollipop stick (or 3 x Bamboo Kebab Sticks glued together)
- Small amount of pink Felt – for cheeks
- Strong Glue
- 2 x ⅜" (9 mm) Safety eyes

FINISHED SIZE
(not including stick)

- Swirl Lollipop - About 7¼" (18.5 cm) diameter
- Round Lollipop - About 6⅔" (17 cm) diameter

Pattern Notes

The Swirl Lollipop consists of two sides, made using a spiral pattern with three colors. The sides are then sewn together, encasing a piece of card or craft foam to maintain the shape.

The Round Lollipop is worked in continuous rounds, holding two strands of yarn together throughout.

Swirl Lollipop

Abbreviations used:

PM – place marker

RM – remove marker

Lollipop Swirl (make 2)

Rnd 1: (Right Side) Using Color A, make a magic ring, *(sc, hdc, 2 dc) in ring, remove hook, PM in last st loop*, (do not close ring), join Color B with sl st to magic ring; repeat from * to * once, (do not close ring); join Color C with sl st to magic ring, repeat from * to * once more; close magic ring. (3 sc, 3 hdc, 6 dc).

Round 1 – Before closing magic ring

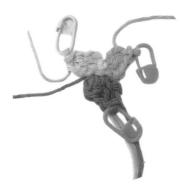

End of Round 1 with magic ring closed

Rnd 2: Starting with Color A, *insert hook in relevant loop (RM), 2 dc in each of the next 4 sts; remove hook and PM in last loop*; repeat from * to * with Color B; repeat from * to * with Color C. (24 dc – 8 dc in each color)

Rnd 3: Starting with Color A, *insert hook in relevant loop (RM), [2 dc in next st, dc in next st] 4 times, remove hook and PM in last loop*; repeat from * to * with Color B; repeat from * to * with Color C. (36 dc – 12 dc in each color)

Rnd 4: Starting with Color A, *insert hook in relevant loop (RM), [2 dc in next st, dc in each of next 2 sts] 4 times, remove hook and PM in last loop*; repeat from * to * with Color B; repeat from * to * with Color C. (48 dc – 16 dc in each color)

End of Round 4 – Showing spiral pattern

Rnd 5: Starting with Color A, *insert hook in relevant loop (RM), [2 dc in next st, dc in each of next 3 sts] 4 times, remove hook and PM in last loop*; repeat from * to * with Color B; repeat from * to * with Color C. (60 dc – 20 dc in each color)

Rnd 6: Starting with Color A, *insert hook in relevant loop (RM), [2 dc in next st, dc in each of next 4 sts] 4 times, remove hook and PM in last loop*; repeat from * to * with Color B; repeat from * to * with Color C. (72 dc – 24 dc in each color)

Rnd 7: Starting with Color A, *insert hook in relevant loop (RM), [2 dc in next st, dc in each of next 5 sts] 3 times, dc in each of next 2 sts, hdc in each of next 2 sts, sc in next st, sl st in next st, fasten off, leaving a long tail for sewing*; repeat from * to * with Color B; repeat from * to * with Color C. (69 dc, 6 hdc, 3 sc, 3 sl sts – 23 dc, 2 hdc, 1 sc, 1 sl st in each color).

Finishing - Use photos as a guide

If using bamboo sticks, glue them together and leave to dry.
With right side of one Lollipop Swirl facing, position and insert Safety Eyes.
Using black embroidery floss or yarn, embroider the mouth using small, straight stitches.
Cut out two small circles of pink Felt for cheeks. Position and sew or glue in place.
Cut a circle of card (or craft foam) to fit Lollipop Swirl
(Note: the shaft of the Safety Eyes might protrude through the card

depending on the length of the shaft.
Position the lollipop stick on card (or craft foam) and glue securely in place. Leave to dry.
Place a thin layer of stuffing on the wrong side of the back Lollipop Swirl. Then place the card with stick on top. Place another layer of stuffing, before positioning the front Lollipop Swirl (with face) on top.
Sew the two Lollipop Swirls together, adding more stuffing if necessary.

Position of Eyes and Mouth

Cut card positioned and glued to Lollipop stick

Shows assembly of all pieces before sewing

Round Lollipop

Rnd 1: (Right Side) Holding 2 strands of Color A together, make a magic ring; 8 sc into the ring. (8 sc) DO NOT JOIN. Mark end of round and move marker each round.
Rnd 2: [2 sc in next st, sc in next st] around. (12 sc)
Rnd 3: [2 sc in next st, sc in next st] around. (18 sc)
Rnd 4: [2 sc in next st, sc in each of next 2 sts] around. (24 sc)
Rnd 5: [2 sc in next st, sc in each of next 2 sts] around. (32 sc)
Rnd 6: [2 sc in next st, sc in each of next 3 sts] around. (40 sc)
Rnd 7: [2 sc in next st, sc in each of next 3 sts] around. (50 sc)
Rnds 8-17: Sc in each st around. (50 sc)

Rnd 18: [Sc2tog, sc in each of next 3 sts] around. (40 sc)
Rnd 19: [Sc2tog, sc in each of next 3 sts] around. (32 sc)
  - Start stuffing, adding more as you go.
Rnd 20: [Sc2tog, sc in each of next 2 sts] around. (24 sc)
Rnd 21: [Sc2tog, sc in each of next 2 sts] around. (18 sc)
Rnd 22: [Sc2tog, sc in next st] around. (12 sc)
Rnd 23: [Sc2tog] around. (6 sc)
Fasten off, leaving a long tail for sewing.

Round 1- Shows using the double strand of yarn

End of Round 23 – stuffed Lollipop (see Finishing for making a hole in the stuffing for inserting stick)

Lollipop Band

Rnd 1: (Right Side) Using double strand Color A, ch 50, taking care not to twist sts, sl st to first ch to make a ring; sc in each ch around. (50 sc) **DO NOT JOIN.** Mark end of round and move marker each round.

Rnds 3–5: Sc in each st around. (50 sc)
At the end of Round 5, sl st in next st, and fasten off leaving long tail for sewing.

Round 1 – Joined ring
of chain stitches

End of Round 5 - Finished band

○○○○○○○○○○○○○○○○○○○○○○○○○○

Finishing - Use photos as a guide

If using bamboo sticks, glue them together and leave to dry.

With right side of Band facing, insert Safety Eyes on Round 3 – about 7 stitches apart.
Using black embroidery floss or yarn, embroider the mouth using small, straight stitches between the eyes.
Cut out two small circles of pink Felt for cheeks. Position and sew or glue in place on Band.

Wrap Band around center of Lollipop and sew in place.
Push lollipop stick up through center of last round to make a hole in the stuffing for it. (Note: the stick needs to be stable, so more stuffing might need to be added around the stick.)
Remove stick and apply glue to tip. Reinsert glued stick into Lollipop.
Glue the last round to the stick at entry point. Leave to dry.
Weave in all ends.

Glued stick inserted into hole
made in lollipop stuffing

Gluing the last round to the lollipop stick

Happy
DONUTS

These cheeky colorful donuts are super happy all the time.
Crocheting them will make you super happy too!

Materials

YARN

Scheepjes Catona 50g
- Main Color (MC): Topaz (179) – 1 ball
- Color A: Tropic (253) - 1 ball
- Color B: Freesia (519) - 1 ball
- Color C: Lavender (520) – 1 ball
- Color D: Old Rose (408) – 1 ball

PLUS

- Size #7 (4.50 mm) crochet hook (or suitable size for yarn used)
- Yarn needle
- Stitch marker/s
- Toy stuffing
- 8 x ¼" (6 mm) Safety Eyes – 2 for each Donut
- Embroidery floss or yarn in four colors (dark pink, yellow, turquoise, mid-pink) for sprinkles

FINISHED SIZE

- Each Donut is about 3½" (9 cm) diameter.

Pattern Notes

Each Donut consists of a base and a top, worked in continuous rounds.
The tops are decorated and then the pieces are sewn together.

Donut Base (make 4 – 1 for each Donut)

Using MC:

Rnd 1: (Right Side) Make a magic ring; 6 sc into ring. (6 sc) DO NOT JOIN. Mark end of round and move marker each round.
Rnd 2: 2 sc in each st around. (12 sc)
Rnd 3: [2 sc in next st, sc in next st] around. (18 sc)
Rnd 4: [2 sc in next st, sc in each of next 2 sts] around. (24 sc)
Rnd 5: [2 sc in next st, sc in each of next 3 sts] around. (30 sc)
Rnd 6: [2 sc in next st, sc in each of next 4 sts] around. (36 sc)
Rnds 7–9: Sc in each st around. (36 sc)
At the end of Round 9, fasten off, leaving a long tail for sewing.

Completed donut base

Donut Tops (make 4 – 1 each in Color A, Color B, Color C & Color D)

Rnds 1–9: Using top color, repeat Rounds 1 to 9 of Donut Base.
At the end of Round 9, there are 36 sc. Fasten off, leaving a long tail for sewing.

Finishing - Use photos as a guide

Using embroidery floss or yarn, embroider different colored sprinkles on the right side of all the Donut Tops.
With right side of Top facing, insert Safety Eyes between Round 6 and Round 7 - about 7 stitches apart. Repeat for other Tops.

Using black embroidery floss or yarn, embroider a happy mouth (between the Eyes) on all Tops Sew a Base and a Top together, stuffing as you go.

Key
LIME PIE

A real favorite, this crochet Key Lime pie will certainly get your mouth watering. It looks so fresh and tangy.. mmmm... Yummy!

Materials

YARN	PLUS	FINISHED SIZE

Scheepjes Catona 50g
- Color A: Topaz (179) – 1 ball
- Color B: Lemon Chiffon (100) – 1 ball
- Color C: Old Lace (130) – 1 ball
- Color D: Green Yellow (245) - small amount for Lime and Strawberry Top

- Yarn and materials for Strawberry (page 110)
- Size D-3 (3.25 mm) crochet hook (or suitable size for yarn used)
- Yarn needle
- Stitch marker/s
- Toy stuffing

- About 4½" (11.5 cm) long, and 3¼" (8.25 cm) high (including twisted lime)

Pattern Notes

The Pie Slice pieces, except the Dollop of Cream, are all worked in rows.
The Dollop of Cream is worked in continuous rounds.

The Lime is worked in un-joined, turned rounds (rows), creating a split. By twisting the ends in opposite directions, the lime has a lovely twisted shape.

Lime Pie Slice

Crust Base

Row 1: (Right Side) Using Color A, ch 3, sc in 2nd ch from hook, sc in last ch. (2 sc)
Row 2: Ch 1, turn, 2 sc in each st across. (4 sc)
Rows 3–4: Ch 1, turn, sc in each st across. (4 sc)
Row 5: Ch 1, turn, 2 sc in first st, [sc in next st] across to last st, 2 sc in last st. (6 sc)
Rows 6–7: Ch 1, turn, sc in each st across. (6 sc)
Rows 8–22: Repeat Rows 5-7 five times.

At the end of Row 22, there are 16 sc.
Row 23: Repeat Row 5. (18 sc)
Row 24: Ch 1, turn, working in **back loops** only, sc in each st across. (18 sc)
Rows 25–30: Ch 1, turn, sc in each st across. (18 sc)
At the end of Row 30, fasten off and weave in ends.

Pie Sides (make 2)

Row 1: (Right Side) Using Color B, ch 23, sc in 2nd ch from hook, sc in each of next 21 ch. (22 sc)
Rows 2–5: Ch 1, turn, sc in each st across. (22 sc)
At the end of Row 5, fasten off.

Pie Topping

Rows 1–23: Using Color B, repeat Rows 1 to 23 of Crust Base.
At the end of Row 23, fasten off, leaving a long tail for sewing.

Dollop of Cream

Rnd 1: (Right Side) Using Color C, make a magic ring, 6 sc into ring. (6 sc) DO NOT JOIN. Mark end of round and move marker each round.
Rnd 2: 2 sc in each st around. (12 sc)
Rnd 3: [2 sc in next st, sc in next st] around. (18 sc)
Rnd 4: [2 sc in next st, sc in each of next 2 sts] around. (24 sc)
Rnd 5: Sc in each st around. (24 sc)
Rnd 6: Dc in each of next 2 sts, 2 dc in each of next 4 sts, dc in each of next 2 sts, sc in each of next 16 st. (12 dc, 16 sc)
Sl st in next st, and fasten off leaving a long tail for sewing.

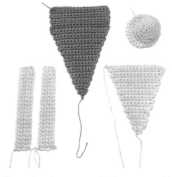

The pie pieces ready for assembly

Lime Slice

Row 1: (Right Side) Using Color D, make a magic ring, 6 sc into ring. (6 sc) Close ring (without joining).
Change to Color B.
Row 2: Ch 1, turn (wrong side facing), 2 sc in each st across. (12 sc)
Row 3: Ch 1, turn, [2 sc in next st, sc in next st] across. (18 sc)
Row 4: Ch 1, turn, [2 sc in next st, sc in each of next 2 sts] across. (24 sc)
Change to Color D.
Row 5: Ch 1, turn, [2 sc in next st, sc in each of next 3 sts] across. (30 sc)
Fasten off and weave in ends.

At the end of Row 5 – With right side facing.

Using Color D, embroider straight lines on both the right and wrong side of the Lime Slice.

Embroidered lines showing segment detail.

Twist the Lime into shape.

Strawberry
Make one complete Strawberry – page 110

⊚⊚⊚⊚⊚⊚⊚⊚⊚⊚⊚⊚⊚⊚⊚⊚⊚⊚⊚⊚⊚

Finishing - Use photos as a guide

Sew the length of each Pie Side to either side of Crust Base, starting from the point. Fold Crust Base along Row 24 and sew the edges of Pie Sides up the Crust Base.
Stuff the pie.
Position and sew the Dollop of Cream to the Pie Topping, stuffing lightly.
Sew the Pie Topping to Sides along the second last row of Crust.
Using Color D, embroider small, straight lines, across Topping and Cream – as lime peel shavings.
Position and sew the twisted Lime Slice and Strawberry on the Topping.
Weave in any ends.

Lemon
SPONGE CAKE

The Lemon Sponge cake looks so delicious and, well...
"Lemony". It makes a lovely little gift. What about using
them as wonderful place-setting name holders on the
poshest of dinner tables? Each guest could take one home as
a keepsake.

Materials

YARN	PLUS	FINISHED SIZE
Scheepjes Catona 50g	⚬ size D-3 (3.25mm) crochet hook (or suitable size for yarn used)	⚬ About 3" (7.5 cm) wide; 3¼" (8.25 cm) long, and 3½" (9 cm) high (including toppings)
⚬ Color A: Lemon Chiffon (100) – 1 ball	⚬ Yarn needle	
⚬ Color B: Lemon (280) – 1 ball	⚬ Stitch marker/s	
⚬ Color C: Old Lace (130) – 1 ball	⚬ Toy stuffing	

Pattern Notes

The Top, Base and Sides of the cake are worked in rows. The cream and lemon decorations are sewn on top on the finished cake.

Cake

Top – Base (make 2)

Row 1: (Right Side) Using Color A, ch 15, sc in 2nd ch from hook, sc in each of next 13 ch. (14 sc)

Rows 2–14: Ch 1, turn, sc in each st across. (14 sc)

At the end of Row 14, fasten off, leaving a long tail for sewing.

Cake Sides

Row 1: (Right Side) Using Color A, ch 57, sc in 2nd ch from hook, sc in each of next 55 ch. (56 sc)

Rows 2–4: Ch 1, turn, sc in each st across. (56 sc)

Change to Color C.

Row 5: Ch 1, turn, sc in each st across. (56 sc)

Change to Color B.

Row 6: Ch 1, turn, sc in each st across. (56 sc)

Change to Color C.

Row 7: Ch 1, turn, sc in each st across. (56 sc)

Change to Color A.

Rows 8–11: Ch 1, turn, sc in each st across. (56 sc)

At the end of Row 11, fasten off, leaving a long tail for sewing.

Cream Topping

Row 1: (Right Side) Using Color C, ch 57, sc in 2nd ch from hook, sc in each of next 55 ch. (56 sc)

Row 2: Ch 3, turn, 3 dc in first st, [4 dc in next st] across. (224 dc)

Fasten off, leaving a long tail for sewing.

Completed cream topping

Lemon Slice (make 2)

Rnd 1: (Right Side) Using Color B, make a magic ring, 6 sc into ring. (6 sc) DO NOT JOIN. Mark end of round and move marker each round.

Change to Color A.

Rnd 2: 2 sc in each st around. (12 sc)

Rnd 3: [2 sc in next st, sc in next st] around. (18 sc)

Rnd 4: [2 sc in next st, sc in each of next 2 sts] around. (24 sc)

Rnd 5: [2 sc in next st, sc in each of next 3 sts] around. (30 sc)

Change to Color B

Rnd 6: [2 sc in next st, sc in each of next 4 sts] around. (36 sc)

Row 7: With right side facing, fold flat circle in half (wrong sides together), ch 1, working through both thicknesses, matching stitches, [sl st in next st] across.

Fasten off and weave in all ends.

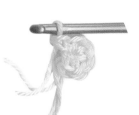

End of Round 1 – Changing color for next round

Round 2 – Made using new color

Before starting Row 7 – Circle folded in half

Row 7 – Working the slip stitches through both thicknesses

Row 7 – Slip stitching across semi-circle

Finishing - Use photos as a guide

Using Color B, embroider long, straight stitches on both sides of Lemon semi-circles, to create segments. Weave in ends.

Sew the edges of the Cake Sides together, matching rows, to form a ring.
Using long pins, mark every 14th st on both edges of Cake Sides ring – these are the corners.

With right side on outside (wrong side inside), position the corners and pin the Cake Base to the bottom edge of Cake Sides ring, and sew in place.
Stuff the Cake.
With right side on outside (wrong side inside), position the Cake Top and sew to top edge of Cake Sides ring.
Position Cream Topping in back and forth rows across Cake Top, and sew in place.
Position and sew the two Lemon Slices in place.

Embroidered lemon slice

Marking out the four corners

Cream sewn on in back and forth rows

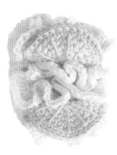

Top view - lemon slices sewn in place

Mr Ginger
THE GINGERBREAD COOKIE

Mr. Ginger is one snappy dresser!

Materials

YARN

Scheepjes Catona 50g
- Color A: Ginger Gold (383) - 1 ball
- Color B: Tropic (253) - small amount for Bow Tie

PLUS

- Size D-3 (3.25 mm) crochet hook (or suitable size for yarn used)
- Yarn needle
- Stitch marker/s
- 5 x mini black Buttons
- Sewing thread & sewing needle (or glue)
- Pink felt – small amount for cheeks

FINISHED SIZE

- About 5" (13 cm) tall.

Pattern Notes

Mr Ginger consists of two complete Cookies, crocheted together.

Instead of using mini-buttons, embroider French knots for the Eyes and front Buttons.

Experiment with different bow tie colors, or make an army of crochet gingerbread biscuits with different color bow ties and buttons and string them together to form a fun yummy looking bunting!

Gingerbread Cookie (Make 2)

First Leg

Row 1: (Wrong Side) Using Color A, ch 3, sc in 2rd chain from the hook, 2 sc in last ch. (3 sc)
Row 2: (Right Side) Ch 1, turn, 2 sc in first st, sc in next st, 2 sc in last st. (5 sc)
Row 3: Ch 1, turn, sc in each st across. (5 sc)
Row 4: Ch 1, turn, 2 sc in first st, [sc in next st] across. (6 sc)
Rows 5–6: Ch 1, turn, sc in each st across. (6 sc)
At the end of Row 6, fasten off.

Second Leg

Rows 1–6: Repeat Rows 1-6 of First Leg.
At the end of Row 6, DO NOT fasten off.
Row 7: (Joining Legs) Ch 1, turn, sc in each st across Second Leg, with wrong side of First Leg facing, working in Row 6, sc in each st across First Leg. (12 sc)

Row 7 – Joining Legs together

Body

Rows 9–12: Ch 1, turn, sc in each st across. (12 sc)
At the end of Row 12, fasten off and weave in all ends.

At the end of Row 12

Arms

Row 13: Using Color A, ch 3, with wrong sides of Legs facing, working in Row 12, sc in each st across. (12 sc & 3 ch)
Row 14: Ch 4, turn, sc in 2rd ch from hook, sc in each of next 2 ch, sc in each of next 12 sts, sc in each of next 3 ch. (18 sc)

Beginning of Row 14 – starting the Arms

Row 15: Ch 1, turn, 2 sc in first st, [sc in next st] across to last st, 2 sc in last st. (20 sc)
Row 16: Ch 1, turn, sc in each st across. (20 sc)
Row 17: Ch 1, turn, sc2tog, [sc in next st] across to last 2 sts, sc2tog. (18 sc)
Row 18: Ch 1, turn, sc in each st across. (18 sc)
Row 19: Ch 1, turn, sc2tog, [sc in next st] across to last 2 sts, sc2tog. (16 sc)
Fasten off and weave in ends.

Head

Row 20: With right side facing, working in Row 19, join Color A with sl st in 7th st, ch 1, 2 sc in each of next 2 sts, sc in next st. (5 sc) Leave remaining 6 sts unworked.

Beginning of Row 20 - Joining yarn for Head.

Row 21: Ch 1, turn, 2 sc in first st, sc in each of next 3 sts, 2 sc in last st. (7 sc)

Row 22: Ch 1, turn, 2 sc in first st, sc in each of next 5 sts, 2 sc in last st. (9 sc)

Row 23: Ch 1, turn, 2 sc in first st, sc in each of next 7 sts, 2 sc in last st. (11 sc)

Row 24: Ch 1, turn, sc in each st across. (11 sc)

Row 25: Ch 1, turn, sc2tog, sc in each of next 7 sts, sc2tog. (9 sc)

Row 26: Ch 1, turn, sc2tog, sc in each of next 5 sts, sc2tog. (7 sc)

Row 27: Ch 1, turn, sc2tog, sc in each of next 3 sts, sc2tog. (5 sc)

Row 28: Ch 1, turn, sc2tog, sc in next st, sc2tog. (3 sc)

Fasten off and weave in ends.

Assembly

Holding both Cookies with wrong sides together, matching stitches and shaping, working through both thicknesses, join Color A with sl st to any point on Cookie, ch 1, sc evenly around outer edge; join with sl st to first sc. Fasten off and weave in ends.

Assembled Body

Bow Tie

Row 1: (Right Side) Using Color B, ch 7, sc in 2nd ch from hook, [sc in next ch] across. (6 sc)

Row 2: Ch 1, turn, sc in each st across. (6 sc).

Fasten off and weave in ends.

End of Row 2

Using a separate piece of Color B, wrap yarn around the center to create the bow tie shape.

Wrapped yarn creating bow tie shape

Finishing – Use photo as guide

Position and sew or glue the Bow Tie in place.
Position the Eyes and Buttons and sew or glue in place.
Cut small circles of pink felt and sew or glue in place.

Mr Ginger is complete!

Pink Swirl

CUPCAKE

A cupcake makes a lovely present or a fun ornament just to sit on your kitchen shelf!

Besides looking yummy, the cupcake can be used as a pin cushion or as a crochet needle and stitch marker holder.

Materials

YARN	PLUS	FINISHED SIZE
Scheepjes Catona 50g	⚙ Size D-3 (3.25 mm) crochet hook (or suitable size for yarn used)	⚙ About 3½" (9 cm) wide
⚙ Main Color (MC): Chrystalline (385) – 1 ball (for Cupcake Case)	⚙ Yarn needle	
⚙ Color A: Hazelnut (503) – small amount for Case	⚙ Stitch marker/s	
⚙ Color B: Marshmallow (518) – 1 ball	⚙ Toy stuffing	
⚙ Color C: Rosewood (258) - small amount for Cherry		

Pattern Notes

The Swirl Topping uses different sized stitches to create the "swirl" effect.

⚙⚙⚙⚙⚙⚙⚙⚙⚙⚙⚙⚙⚙⚙⚙⚙⚙⚙⚙⚙⚙⚙⚙⚙⚙⚙

Special Stitches

Shallow Front Post Single Crochet (S-FPsc): Insert hook from front to back under the two loops of specified stitch (as you would for a normal stitch), then insert hook from back to front under the two loops of the next stitch, pull up a loop (2 loops on hook), yarn over and draw through both loops on hook.

Note: Instead of working around the post of stitches, the shallow post stitch is worked around at the top of the stitches, inserting your hook as you would for a normal stitch.

⚙⚙⚙⚙⚙⚙⚙⚙⚙⚙⚙⚙⚙⚙⚙⚙⚙⚙⚙⚙⚙⚙⚙⚙⚙⚙

Cupckae Case

Using MC, make one complete Cupcake Case – page 112

⚙⚙⚙⚙⚙⚙⚙⚙⚙⚙⚙⚙⚙⚙⚙⚙⚙⚙⚙⚙⚙⚙⚙⚙⚙⚙

Cupcake Sides

Rnd 1: With right side of Cupcake Case facing, join Color A with sl st to any inside st on Round 10 (see arrow in photo), [sc in next st] around. (41 sc) DO NOT JOIN. Mark end of round.

Rnd 2: Sc in each st around. (41 sc)
Sl st in next st, and fasten off, weaving in all ends.

Arrow indicates the inside stitches on Round 10

Working Round 1 in the stitches on Round 10

End of Round 2

Side view of Cupcake Case with Sides

⚙⚙⚙⚙⚙⚙⚙⚙⚙⚙⚙⚙⚙⚙⚙⚙⚙⚙⚙⚙⚙⚙⚙⚙⚙⚙

Swirl Topping

Row 1: (Right Side – First Section) Using Color B, ch 17, sl st in 8th ch from hook; sc in next ch, hdc in next ch, dc in next ch, 2 dc in next ch, dc in next ch, 2 tr in next ch, tr in next ch, 2 dtr in next ch, dtr in last ch. (12 sts, ch-7 ring)

Row 2: (Wrong Side) Ch 1, turn, S-FPsc in first st, [S-FPsc in next st] across, sl st in ring. (11 S-FPsc & sl st)

Row 3: (Next Section) Ch 1, turn, sc in first st, hdc in next st, dc in next st, 2 dc in next st, dc in next st, 2 tr in next st, tr in next st, 2 dtr in next st, dtr in the next st. Leave remaining 2 sts unworked. (12 sts)

Row 4: Ch 1, turn, [S-FPsc in next st] across, sl st in ring. (11 S-FPsc & sl st)

Rows 5–20: Repeat Rows 3 to 4.

At the end of Row 20, there are 10 sections. Fasten off, leaving a long tail for sewing.

End of Row 1 – First Section

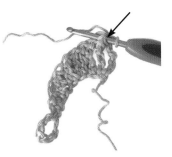

Start of Row 2 – Arrow
showing insertion point for
Shallow-Front Post Single
Crochet.

End of Row 2 - before final
slip stitch into the chain ring

Row 3 – Start of the next
section

End of Row 3 – Leaving the
last two stitches unworked

Cherry

Rnd 1: (Right Side) Using Color C, make a magic ring, 6 sc into ring. (6 sc) DO NOT JOIN. Mark end of round and move marker each round.
Rnd 2: 2 sc in each st around. (12 sc)
Rnd 3: Sc in each st around. (12 sc)

Rnd 4: Sc2tog around. (6 sc)
Fasten off leaving long tail for sewing.

Stuff lightly.

Finishing - Use photos as a guide

⬡ Swirl Topping – Using long tail and yarn needle, sew end of section 10 to starting chain.
⬡ Insert stuffing in Cupcake base and Swirl Topping.
⬡ Position and pin Swirl Topping to Cupcake Sides and sew in place.

⬡ Cherry - Using long tail and yarn needle, weave tail through the front loops of stitches on the last round, and pull tight to close.
⬡ Sew Cherry on the top.

View from top of completed
Swirl Topping

Stuffing inserted into both parts

Swirl Topping pinned in place
and ready to sew

Rainbow
CAKE

Life's a rainbow! Well it certainly is with this Rainbow Cake in your life! You'll love crocheting this colorful, over-sized slice of cake...

Materials

YARN

Scheepjes Catona 50g
- Color A: Old Lace (130) – 1 ball
- Color B: Ultra Violet (282) – 1 ball
- Color C: Tropic (253) – 1 ball
- Color D: Lime (512) – 1 ball
- Color E: Lemon (280) – 1 ball
- Color F: Freesia (519) – 1 ball

PLUS

- Yarn and materials for Strawberry (page 110) and Kiwi Fruit Slice (page 111)
- Size D-3 (3.25 mm) crochet hook (or suitable size for yarn used)
- Yarn needle
- Stitch marker/s
- Toy stuffing

FINISHED SIZE

- About 6" (15.25 cm) wide (at widest point), 6½" (16.5 cm) long; and about 4¼" (10.8 cm) high.

Pattern Notes

The main parts of the Cake are worked in rows. The Cake Decorations are sewn on afterwards.

Special Stitches

Popcorn Stitch (pc): Work 5 double crochets in the stitch specified. Remove the hook from the loop. Insert hook in first double crochet made, place loop back on hook and pull through the stitch. Ch 1 to secure.

Rainbow Cake

Frosting

Using Color A:

Row 1: (Right Side) Ch 3, sc in 2nd ch from hook, sc in last ch. (2 sc)

Row 2: Ch 1, turn, 2 sc in each st across. (4 sc)

Row 3: Ch 1, turn, sc in each st across. (4 sc)

Row 4: Ch 1, turn, 2 sc in first st, [sc in next st] across to last st, 2 sc in last st. (6 sc)

Rows 5–22: Repeat Rows 3 to 4 nine times.
At the end of Row 22, there are 24 sc.

Rows 23–24: Ch 1, turn, sc in each st across. (24 sc)

Row 25: Ch 1, turn, 2 sc in first st, [sc in next st] across to last st, 2 sc in last st. (26 sc)

Rows 26–28: Ch 1, turn, sc in each st across. (26 sc)

Row 29: Ch 2, turn, [pc in next st, ch 1, skip next st] 12 times, pc in last st. (13 popcorns)

Fasten off, leaving a long tail for sewing.

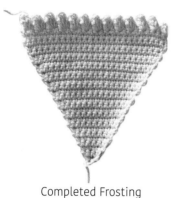

Completed Frosting

Cake Base

Rows 1–28: Using Color B, repeat Rows 1 to 28 of Frosting.

Row 29: Ch 1, turn, sc in each st across. (26 sc)

Fasten off, leaving a long tail for sewing.

Cake Filling

Row 1: (Right Side) Using Color B, ch 57, sc in 2nd ch from hook, sc in each of next 55 ch. (56 sc)

Row 2: Ch 1, turn, sc in each st across. (56 sc)

Rows 3–23: Repeat Row 2, changing color as follows:

Color B - 3 rows (Row 1-Row 3)

Color A - 2 rows

Color C - 3 rows

Color A - 2 rows

Color D - 3 rows

Color A - 2 rows

Color E - 3 rows

Color A - 2 rows

Color F - 3 rows

At the end of Row 23, fasten off and weave in all ends.

End of Row 23, before
weaving in ends

Cream Side

Row 1: (Wrong Side) Using Color A, ch 27, 2 sc in 2nd ch from hook, sc in each of next 25 ch. (26 sc)

Row 2: (Right Side) Ch 1, turn, sc in first st, [pc in next st, sc in next st] across, ending with pc in last st. (13 popcorns)

Row 3: Ch 1, turn, sc in each st across. (26 sc)

Rows 4–19: Repeat Rows 2 to 3 eight times.

Row 20: Ch 1, turn, sc in each st across. (26 sc)

Fasten off, leaving a long tail for sewing.

Cream Side Row 10 – Making the popcorn

Assembly - Use photos as a guide

Mark the center of the Cake Filling strip on both the bottom edge (Color B) and last row (Color F).

With right sides facing outwards, position Row 1 of Frosting to marked center on last row of Cake Filling. Position either end of the last row of Frosting to the edges of Cake Filling and sew in place.

Position and sew the Cream Side to the Topping and sides of Cake Filling. Turn upside down and stuff cavity.

Position Row 1 of Cake Base to marked center of Cake Filling and sew around.

Weave in all ends.

Cake Base positioned to center of Cake Filling before being sewn in place.

○○○○○○○○○○○○○○○○○○○○○

Cake Decorations

Rainbow (make 3)

Rnd 1: (Right Side) Using Color B, make a magic ring, 6 sc into ring; join with sl st to first sc. (6 sc) Fasten off and weave in all ends.

Rnd 2: Join Color C with sl st to any stitch, ch 1, 2 sc in same st as joining, [2 sc in next st] around; join with sl st to first sc. (12 sc) Fasten off and weave in all ends.

Rnd 3: Join Color D with sl st to any stitch, ch 1, 2 sc in same st as joining, sc in next st, [2 sc in next st, sc in next st] around; join with sl st to first sc. (18 sc) Fasten off and weave in all ends.

Rnd 4: Join Color E with sl st to any stitch, ch 1, 2 sc in same st as joining, sc in each of next 2 sts, [2 sc in next st, sc in each of next 2 sts] around; join with sl st to first sc. (24 sc) Fasten off and weave in all ends.

Rnd 5: Join Color F with sl st to any stitch, ch 1, 2 sc in same st as joining, sc in each of next 3 sts, [2 sc in next st, sc in each of next 3 sts] around; join with sl st to first sc. (30 sc) DO NOT FASTEN OFF.

Row 6: With right side facing, fold flat circle in half (wrong sides together), ch 1, working through both thicknesses, matching stitches, [sl st in next st] across.
Fasten off and weave in all ends.

End of Round 4
(ends not woven in yet)

Row 6 – Working slip stitches through both thicknesses

○○○○○○○○○○○○○○○○○○○○○

Strawberry
Make one complete Strawberry – page 110

Kiwi Fruit Slice
Make one complete Kiwi Fruit Slice – page 111

Finishing - Use photos as a guide

Using Colors B to F, embroider small, straight stitches on Frosting – as sprinkles.

Position the 3 Rainbows into the ridge (behind popcorn row on Frosting), overlapping slightly, and sew in place.

Position and sew (or glue) the Strawberry and Kiwi Fruit on the Frosting.

Weave in all ends.

Side view – Showing ridge where Rainbows are positioned

The Rainbows are sewn in place

Rose
CUPCAKE

Such decadence! The shaded petal detail adds real elegant beauty to this cupcake. It could be a Mother's Day gift or a birthday gift for a special lady who loves roses.

Materials

YARN	PLUS	FINISHED SIZE
Scheepjes Catona 50g ◉ Main Color (MC): Lemonade (403) – 1 ball (for Cupcake Case) ◉ Color A: Old Lace (130) – 1 ball ◉ Color B: Lime (512) - small amount for Leaves	◉ Size D-3 (3.25 mm) crochet hook (or suitable size for yarn used) ◉ Yarn needle ◉ Stitch marker/s ◉ Toy stuffing ◉ Dark green embroidery floss or yarn - for Leaf striation detail ◉ Blusher and small blusher brush – for shading petals	◉ About 2⅔" (7 cm) high and 4½" (11.5 cm) at widest point (including Leaves).

Pattern Notes

The first part of the Rose Topping is worked in continuous rounds – only in the back loops. The "petals" are then worked in the unused front loops, in a continuous spiral - from the center outwards.

Cupcake Case

Using MC, make one complete Cupcake Case – page 112

Topping

Rnd 1: (Right Side) Using Color A, make a magic ring, 6 sc into ring. (6 sc) DO NOT JOIN. Mark end of round and move marker each round.

Rnd 2: Working in **back loops** only, [2 sc in next st] around. (12 sc)

Hint: Mark the first unused front loop (with a different color marker) for joining the Rose Detail later.

Rnd 3: Working in **back loops** only, [2 sc in next st, sc in next st] around. (18 sc)

Rnd 4: Working in **back loops** only, [2 sc in next st, sc in each of next 2 sts] (24 sc)

Rnd 5: Working in **back loops** only, [2 sc in next st, sc in each of next 3 sts] around. (30 sc)

Rnd 6: Working in **back loops** only, [2 sc in next st, sc in each of next 4 sts] around. (36 sc)

Rnd 7: Working in **back loops** only, [2 sc in next st, sc in each of next 5 sts] around. (42 sc)

Rnd 8: Working in **back loops** only, [2 sc in next st, sc in each of next 6 sts] around. (48 sc)

Rnds 9-10: Working in both loops, sc in each st around. (48 sc)

Rnd 11: [Sc2tog, sc in each of next 6 sts] around. (42 sts)

Rnd 12: [Sc2tog, sc in each of next 5 sts] around. (36 sts)

Fasten off, leaving a long tail for sewing.

Rose Detail

With right side of Topping facing, join Color A with sl st to first unused front loop (marked st), ch 1, sc in same st as joining, following the spiral, [dc in next lp, 2 dc in next lp] around to last lp at end of Round 7.

Fasten off and weave in all ends.

At the end of Round 8, with 7 rounds of unused front loops showing

Rose Detail – Joining to the first unused front loop at center of Topping

Working the double crochets in the front loops, creating a raised spiral

Rose Leaf (make 2)

Using Color B, ch 7, sl st in 2nd ch from hook, sc in next ch, hdc in next ch, 2 dc in each of next 2 ch, 7 tr in last ch; working in unused lps on other side of starting ch, 2 dc in each of next 2 ch, hdc in next ch, sc in last ch; join with sl st to first sl st.

Fasten off and weave in all ends.
Using dark green embroidery floss or yarn, embroider leaf striations using straight stitches on both leaves.

Completed Leaf before ends woven in.

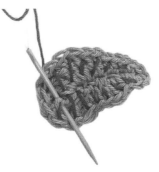

Embroidering the striations on the Leaf.

Finishing - Use photos as a guide

◉ Stuff Cupcake Case and the Topping.
◉ Position and sew the Topping to the inside stitches on Round 10 of Cupcake Case.
◉ Position and sew on Leaves.

◉ Randomly tack down stitches on the outer petal frill in a few places to add shaping.
◉ Apply blusher to edges of Rose Detail (optional).

Arrows show where outer petal is stitched down

Applying blusher on edges of Rose detail.

Top view of finished Cupcake

81

FRUIT DESSERT

Wow your guests with this dessert as your table centerpiece. It looks so delicious, that Penny Baker snuck into the kitchen to have a taste... She just couldn't resist those strawberries!

Materials

YARN	PLUS	FINISHED SIZE
Scheepjes Cahlista 50g	◉ Yarn and materials for Strawberry (page 110) and Kiwi Fruit Slice (page 111)	◉ About 7½" (19 cm) diameter; about 3½" (9 cm) high (including toppings).
◉ Color A: Topaz (179) – 1 ball	◉ Size #7 (4.50 mm) and size D-3 (3.25 mm) crochet hooks (or suitable size for yarn used)	
Color B: Old Lace (130) – 1 ball	◉ Yarn needle	
Scheepjes Catona 50g	◉ Stitch marker/s	
◉ Color C: Old Lace (130) – 1 ball	◉ Toy stuffing	

Pattern Notes

The Pastry Base and Topping are worked in continuous rounds, with the toppings then sewn on top.

Pastry Base

Rnd 1: (Right Side) Using Color A and larger hook, make a magic ring, 6 sc into ring. (6 sc). DO NOT JOIN. Mark end of round and move marker each round.

Rnd 2: 2 sc in each st around. (12 sc)

Rnd 3: [2 sc in next st, sc in next st] around. (18 sc)

Rnd 4: [2 sc in next st, sc in each of next 2 sts] around. (24 sc)

Rnd 5: [2 sc in next st, sc in each of next 3 sts] around. (30 sc)

Rnd 6: [2 sc in next st, sc in each of next 4 sts] around. (36 sc)

Rnd 7: [2 sc in next st, sc in each of next 5 sts] around. (42 sc)

Rnd 8: [2 sc in next st, sc in each of next 6 sts] around. (48 sc)

Rnd 9: [2 sc in next st, sc in each of next 7 sts] around. (54 sc)

Rnd 10: [2 sc in next st, sc in each of next 8 sts] around. (60 sc)

Rnd 11: [2 sc in next st, sc in each of next 9 sts] around. (66 sc)

Rnd 12: [2 sc in next st, sc in each of next 10 sts] around. (72 sc)

Rnd 13: [2 sc in next st, sc in each of next 11 sts] around. (78 sc)

Rnd 14: [2 sc in next st, sc in each of next 12 sts] around. (84 sc)

Rnd 15: [2 sc in next st, sc in each of next 13 sts] around. (90 sc)

Rnd 16: [2 sc in next st, sc in each of next 14 sts] around. (96 sc)

Rnd 17: Working in **back loops** only, sc in each st around. (96 sc)

Rnd 18: Working in both loops, sc in each st around. (96 sc)

Rnd 19: [Sc2tog, sc in each of next 14 sts] around. (90 sc)

Rnd 20: Sc in each st around. (90 sc)

Rnd 21: [Sc2tog, sc in each of next 13 sts] around. (84 sc)

Rnd 22: Sc in each st around. (84 sc)

Rnd 23: [Sc2tog, sc in each of next 12 sts] around. (78 sc)
Fasten off and weave in ends.

Stuff Pastry Base.

Round 11 – The flat circle is growing

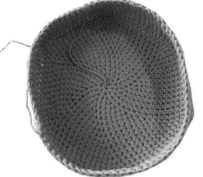

At the end of Round 23 – The finished Pastry Base

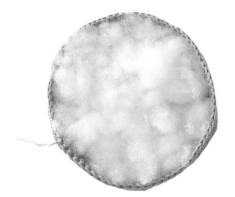

Stuffing the Base

◦◦◦◦◦◦◦◦◦◦◦◦◦◦◦◦◦◦◦◦◦◦◦◦◦◦

Topping
Cream Layer

Rnds 1–13: Using Color B and larger hook, repeat Rounds 1 to 13 of Dessert Bowl.
At the end of Round 13, there are 78 sc. Do not fasten off.

Joining Rnd: Holding Cream Layer and Dessert Bowl with wrong sides together, working through both thicknesses, matching stitches, ch 1, sc in each sc around; join with sl st to first sc. Fasten off and weave in ends.

Joining Round - Crocheting Cream Topping to Pastry Base

Finished Pastry Base with Cream Topping

Cream Swirls (make 12)

Rnd 1: (Right Side) Using Color C and smaller hook, make a magic ring, 4 sc into ring. (4 sc). DO NOT JOIN. Mark end of round and move marker each round.

Rnd 2: 2 sc in each st around. (8 sc)

Rnd 3: Working in **back loops** only, 2 sc in each st around. (16 sc)

Rnd 4: [Sc2tog, sc in next st] 5 times, sc in last st. (11 sc)

Rnd 5: Working in **back loops** only, 2 sc in each st around. (22 sc)

Rnd 6: [Sc2tog, sc in next st] 7 times, sc in last st. (15 sc)

Fasten off, leaving a long tail for sewing.

Stuff all the Cream Swirls.

Round 5 – Working two single crochets in the back loops

Strawberry

Make 12 complete Strawberries – page 110

Kiwi Fruit Slice

Make 12 complete Kiwi Fruit Slices – page 111

Finishing - Use photos as a guide

Position Cream Swirls evenly around outer edge of Cream Topping and sew in place.

Position Strawberries and Kiwi Fruits in center of Cream Topping and sew in place.

Hint: If the Dessert is not for children to play with, instead of sewing, you could glue the pieces in place.

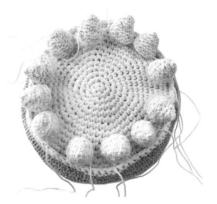

Cream Swirls arranged around the Cream Topping

Jelly
ROLLS

A crochet bakery is only complete when you've got Jelly Rolls. These ones won't even turn your belly to jelly!

Materials

YARN

Scheepjes Catona 50g
- Color A: Topaz (179) – 1 ball
- Color B: Marshmallow (518) – 1 ball
- Color C: Primrose (522) – 1 ball
- Color D: Scarlett (192) – small amount for Jelly Swirl
- Color E: Old Lace (130) – small amount for Cream Swirl

PLUS

- Size D-3 (3.25 mm) crochet hook (or suitable size for yarn used)
- Yarn needle
- Stitch marker/s
- Toy stuffing
- Card (optional)

FINISHED SIZE

- About 2⅔" (7 cm) diameter.

Pattern Notes

The Cake Roll Sides are worked in continuous rounds and then decorated with Surface Slip Stitches.

Note: The card is used to provide stability to the Jelly Rolls. Do not use card if these are to be used as children's toys, so that the Jelly Rolls can be laundered.

Special Stitches

Surface Slip Stitches: Without a loop on hook, insert hook from front (right side) to back (wrong side) in specified start position.

Keeping the working yarn at the back, place a slip knot on hook and pull the loop of the slip knot through to the front, keeping the knot at the back (1 loop on hook).

*Insert hook in next specified position from front to back and pull up a loop through the fabric and through the loop on the hook (slip stitch made). Repeat from * as instructed. For the last stitch, remove hook from loop. Insert hook from back to front in the last spot specified and place loop back on hook, pulling loop through to back.

Cake Roll (make 3 – 1 in each in Color A, Color B & Color C)

First Side

Rnd 1: (Right Side) Using any Color, make a magic ring, 6 sc into ring. (6 sc). DO NOT JOIN. Mark end of round and move marker each round.

Rnd 2: 2 sc in each st around. (12 sc)

Rnd 3: [2 sc in next st, sc in next st] around. (18 sc)

Rnd 4: [2 sc in next st, sc in each of next 2 sts] around. (24 sc)

Rnd 5: [2 sc in next st, sc in each of next 3 sts] around. (30 sc)

Rnd 6: [2 sc in next st, sc in each of next 4 sts] around. (36 sc)

Rnd 7: [2 sc in next st, sc in each of next 5 sts] around. (42 sc)

Rnd 8: Working in **back loops** only, sc in each st around. (42 sc)

Rnds 9–11: Working in both loops, sc in each st around. (42 sc) At the end of Round 11, sl st in next st, and fasten off leaving long tail for sewing.

Second Side

Rnds 1–7: Using same Color, repeat Rounds 1 to 7 of First Side. At the end of Round 7, there are 42 sc. Sl st in next st, and fasten off leaving long tail for sewing.

Jelly and Cream Swirl Decoration

(using Surface Slip Stitches)

For Jelly – Using Color D:

With right side of any Side facing, start the Surface Slip Stitches between any 2 sts on Round 1; working in the spaces between the stitches, follow a swirl pattern (leaving an open round between swirls) around until about Round 7 (about 55 sl sts). Bring loop to back and fasten off.

For Cream – Using Color E: Repeat from * to * on same Side using the same spaces for the slip stitches.

Repeat the Jelly and Cream slip stitches on all six Sides.

Start the swirl by pulling the loop to the front (keeping knot at back).

Creative the Jelly spiral Swrill shape with the surface slip.

Working the Cream swirl in the same spaces as the Jelly swirl.

Wrong Side – Pulling loop through to back to fasten off.

The Jelly and Cream Swirls complete.

Finishing - Use photos as a guide

Cut out six circles of card to fit in the base of the First Side pieces (optional).

Insert cards in base of First Side pieces and stuff. Place another card piece on top and with right sides facing, sew Second Side to First Side.

All the pieces ready for sewing together

Wedding Cake
HANGING CHARM

A Hanging Charm makes a wonderful gift for Bridesmaids! Why not change the color-way to match your own wedding party décor?

These Charms also make lovely wedding table decorations!

Attach a Charm to your wedding gift - for added splendour and decorative charm! And what about making one for a lovely anniversary gift?

Materials

YARN	PLUS	FINISHED SIZE
Scheepjes Catona 50g ◉ Color A: Powder Pink (238) – 1 ball ◉ Color B: Soft Rose (409) – small amount required ◉ Color C: Lime (512) – 1 ball ◉ Color D: Shocking Pink (114) - small amount required	◉ Size D-3 (3.25 mm) crochet hook (or suitable size for yarn used) ◉ Yarn needle ◉ Stitch marker/s ◉ Toy stuffing	◉ About 6" (15 cm) wide (at widest point); about 7" (18 cm) high (excluding hanger).

Pattern Notes

The Charm consists of two crocheted sides. Embellishments are added to each, before crocheting together, adding a floral top hanger piece.

Bobble Rows are worked on the wrong side, for the bobbles to appear on the right side.

Special Stitches

Bobble (with 4 dc) (bob): Yarn over, insert hook in stitch or space specified and pull up a loop (3 loops on hook), yarn over, draw through 2 loops on hook (2 loops remain on hook); [yarn over, insert hook in same stich and pull up a loop, yarn over, draw through 2 loops on hook] 3 times more (5 loops on hook); yarn over, draw through remaining 5 loops. Ch 1 to secure.

Wedding Cake (make 2)

Row 1: (Wrong Side) Using Color A, ch 29, sc in 2nd ch from hook, sc in each of next 27 ch. (28 sc)

Row 2 (Right Side): Ch 1, turn, sc in each st across. (28 sc)

Hint: Place a marker in row 2 to denote right side.

Rows 3–8: Ch 1, turn, sc in each st across. (28 sc)

Row 9: Ch 2 (does NOT count as first dc), turn, bob in first st, [ch 1, skip next st, bob in next st] 13 times, dc in last st. (14 bobbles, 13 ch-1 sps, 1 dc)

Fasten off and weave in all ends.

Row 10: With right side facing, join with sl st to top of 2nd bobble, ch 1, [sc in next ch-1 sp, sc in next bob] 10 times, sc in next ch-1 sp. (21 sc) Leave remaining 4 sts unworked.

Rows 11–18: Ch 1, turn, sc in each st across. (21 sc)

Row 19: Ch 2, turn, bob in first st, [ch 1, skip next st, bob in next st] 9 times, ch 1, skip next, dc in last st. (10 bobbles, 10 ch-1 sps, 1 dc)

Fasten off and weave in all ends.

Row 20: With right side facing, join with sl st to top of 2nd bobble, ch 1, [sc in next ch-1 sp, sc in next bob] 7 times. (14 sc) Leave remaining 4 sts unworked.

Rows 21–28: Ch 1, turn, sc in each st across. (14 sc)

Row 29: Ch 2, turn, bob in first st, [ch 1, skip next st, bob in next st] 6 times, dc in last st. (7 bobbles, 6 ch-1 sps, 1 dc)

At the end of first Wedding Cake, fasten off and weave in all ends. DO NOT FASTEN OFF at end of second Wedding Cake.

Row 9 – Working the final step of the second bobble – ready to yarn over and pull through all loops on hook.

Row 10 – Joining yarn to top of second bobble. (the marker denotes the Right Side)

Row 10 – At the end of row, leaving the last four stitches unworked

Row 20 – With right side facing (marker visible), joining yarn to second bobble

Embellishments

Chain Loops

Bottom Tier: With right side facing, join Color B with sl st to base of first Bobble, [ch 5, sl st at base of next bobble] across row. (13 loops) Fasten off and weave in all ends.

Middle Tier: Repeat Bottom Tier. (9 loops)

Top Tier: Repeat Bottom Tier. (6 loops)

Little Dots

Using Color D, embroider a French Knot above each Bobble on every tier.

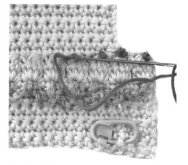

Joining yarn at base of first bobble to start Chain Loops

Slip stitch at base of next bobble to make first Chain Loop

Embroidering French Knots above each bobble

Floral Top (with Hanger)

Note: If you prefer not to have a hanger, omit the ch 20 at beginning of Row 7.

Rnd 1: (Right Side) Using Color C, make a magic ring, 6 sc into ring. (6 sc) DO NOT JOIN. Mark end of round and move marker each round.

Rnd 2: 2 sc in each st around. (12sc)

Rnd 3: [2 sc in next st, sc in next st] around. (18sc)

Rnd 4: [2 sc in next st, sc in each of next 2 sts] around. (24 sc)

Rnd 5: [2 sc in next st, sc in each of next 3 sts] around. (30 sc)

Rnd 6: [2 sc in next st, sc in each of next 4 sts] around. (36 sc)

Row 7: Ch 20, sc in each of the next 8 sts. (8 sc, ch-20 loop) Fasten off, leaving a long tail for sewing.

Fold Floral Top in half, with the hanger in center of semi-circle, and sew the two sides together.

Finished Floral Top,
showing where to fold before sewing

fold line

○○○○○○○○○○○○○○○○○○○○○○○○○

Flower (make 8)

Rnd 1: (Right Side) Using Color B, make a magic ring, 6 sc into ring. (6 sc) Close ring and join with sl st to first sc. Fasten off, leaving a long tail for sewing.

With right side facing, using Color D, embroider 3 French Knots in center of Flower.

Embroidering French Knots

Rose (make 4)

Using Color D, ch 10, sc in 2nd ch from hook, sc in each of next 8 ch. Fasten off, leaving a long tail for sewing.

Curl Rose into shape and secure with a few stitches.

Rose curled into shape

Securing the Rose shape with a few stitches

○○○○○○○○○○○○○○○○○○○○○○○

Assembly - Use photos as a guide

Joining Round: With right side of both Wedding Cakes facing (wrong sides together), place hook in end loop of second Wedding Cake, ch 1, working through both thicknesses, matching stitches and shaping, evenly sc around, working 3 sc in each corner, stuffing lightly as you go; join with sl st to first sc. Fasten off and weave in all ends.

Sew Flowers and Roses to both sides of Floral Top.

Position flat edge of Floral Top at center of top tier and sew in place.

Weave in all ends.

Floral Top sewn to top tier of Wedding Cake

Dollhouse

PENNY BAKER

Penny Baker is always very, very busy and she loves her job!
She makes each and every cake for the Dollhouse Bakery and she's
extremely proud of it.

Materials

YARN

Scheepjes Catona 50g
- Color A: Soft Rose (409) - 1 ball
- Color B: Old Lace (130) - 1 ball
- Color C: English Tea (404) - 1 ball
- Color D: Hazelnut (503) – 1 ball

PLUS

- Size D-3 (3.25mm) crochet hook (or suitable size for yarn used)
- Yarn needle
- Stitch marker/s
- Toy stuffing
- Beige felt – small amount for Face
- Dark brown sewing thread and needle (to embroider Eyes and Mouth and to sew Felt Face onto Head)
- Blusher and blusher brush (to add the rosy cheeks)

- Non-toxic toy filling beads or alternative (Optional - aids Doll to stand, by providing a heavier base)
- Card – small amount for stability of base

FINISHED SIZE

- About 6" (15.2 cm) tall, including her hat. (Doll is suitable for $1/12^{th}$ scale dollhouse

Pattern Notes

⚙ Doll is made by working in continuous rounds.

⚙ Card and toy filling beads are used in bottom section of Body, so that the Doll stands.

⚙ If the beads are small enough to leak through the crochet fabric, place them in a small bag or piece of hosiery before inserting into the Doll.

(Do not use the Beads or Card if the Doll is intended for children.)

⊙⊙⊙⊙⊙⊙⊙⊙⊙⊙⊙⊙⊙⊙⊙⊙⊙⊙⊙⊙⊙⊙⊙⊙⊙⊙

Body

Rnd 1: (Right Side) Starting at the base, using Color A, ch 5, sc in 2nd ch from hook, sc in each of next 2 chs, 3 sc in last ch, working in unused lps on other side of starting ch, sc in each of next 2 chs, 2 sc in last ch. (10 sc) DO NOT JOIN. Mark end of round and move marker each round.

Rnd 2: 2 sc in next st, sc in each of next 2 sts, 2 sc in each of next 3 sts, sc in each of next 2 sts, 2 sc in each of next 2 sts. (16 sc)

Rnd 3: Working in back loops only, sc in each st around (16 sc)

Rnds 4–18: Sc in each st around (16 sc)
At the end of Round 18, change to Color B.

⚙ Cut card to fit into oval base.

⚙ Insert card in base and fill halfway up with beads (if using - see Pattern Notes).

⚙ Start stuffing base and continue stuffing as you go.

Rnds 19–27: Sc in each st around (16 sc)

Rnd 28: *Sc in each of next 4 sts, [sc2tog] twice; repeat from * once more. (12 sc)

Rnd 29: [Sc in each of next 4 sts, sc2tog] twice. (10 sc)
Fasten off leaving long tail for sewing.
Finish stuffing Body.
Using long tail and yarn needle, sew the top edge together.

End of Round 2.
(This can be used as the oval template.)

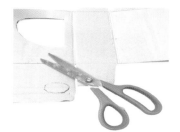

Cut card to fit oval shape at base

After Round 18 - Inserting stuffing

Complete Body

⊙⊙⊙⊙⊙⊙⊙⊙⊙⊙⊙⊙⊙⊙⊙⊙⊙⊙⊙⊙⊙⊙⊙⊙⊙

Arm (Make 2)

Rnd 1: (Right Side) Using Color C, make a magic ring; 6 sc into ring. (6 sc) DO NOT JOIN. Mark end of round and move marker each round.

Rnd 2: Sc in each st around. (6 sc)
Change to Color B.

Rnds 3–13: Sc in each st around. (6 sc)
Fasten off leaving long tail for sewing.
(Note: Arms do not require stuffing).

Changing to Color B at the end of rnd 2.

Finished Arm

Head
Front of Head
Rnd 1: (Right Side) Using Color C, make a magic ring; 6 sc into ring. (6 sc) DO NOT JOIN. Mark end of round and move marker each round.

Rnd 2: 2 sc in each st around. (12 sc)

Rnd 3: [2 sc in next st, sc in next st] around. (18 sc)

Rnd 4: [2 sc in next st, sc in each of next 2 sts] around. (24 sc)
Fasten off leaving a long tail for crocheting.

Back of Head
Rnd 1-4: Using Color D, repeat Rounds 1 to 4 of front of Head. DO NOT FASTEN OFF.

Color C fastened off. Color D not fastened off.

Joining Rnd: With wrong sides of Front and Back together, with Back of Head facing, position Color C tail on opposite side of Color D tail; working through both thicknesses, with Color D, sc in each of next 12 sts (or until you reach Color C tail), change to Color C, sc in each of remaining sts; join with sl st to first sc. Fasten off and weave in all ends.

Line up tails at either side as per arrows

Working in Color D through both thicknesses

Front of Head

Back of Head

Hair Bun (make 2)
Rnd 1: (Right Side) Using Color D, make a magic ring; 6 sc into ring. (6 sc) DO NOT JOIN. Mark end of round and move marker each round.

Rnd 2: [2 sc in next st, sc in next st] around. (9 sc)

Rnd 3: Sc in each st around. (9 sc)

Rnd 4: [Sc2tog, sc in next st] around. (6 sc)
Fasten off leaving a long tail for sewing.

Stuff lightly.

Baker's Hat
Rnd 1: (Right Side) Using Color B, ch 14, join with sl st to first ch to form a ring; sc in each ch around. (14 sc) DO NOT JOIN. Mark end of round and move marker each round.

Rnd 2: [Sc2tog, sc in each of next 2 sts] 3 times, sc2tog. (10 sc)

Rnd 3: [2 sc in next st, sc in next st] around. (15 sc)

Rnd 4: Sc in each st around. (15 sc)

Rnd 5: [Sc2tog, sc in next st] around. (10 sc)

Rnd 6: [Sc2tog] around. (5 sc)
Fasten off leaving a long tail.

Using tail and yarn needle, weave through stitches of last round. Pull tight and bring tail through center of Round 6 to wrong side. Pull to one side to create hat shape (see arrow in photo) and stitch to secure.

Stitch from center to side

Completed Baker's Hat shape

Apron

Row 1: (Right Side) Using Color C, ch 11, sc in 2nd ch from hook, sc in each of next 9 ch. (10 sc)

Row 2: Ch 1, turn, sc in each st across. (10 sc) Change to Color B.

Rows 3–4: Ch 1, turn, sc in each st across. (10 sc) At the end of Row 4, change to Color C.

Rows 5–6: Ch 1, turn, sc in each st across. (10 sc) At the end of Row 6, change to Color B.

Rows 7–10: Repeat Rows 3 to 6. At the end of Row 10, change to Color B.

Row 11: Ch 1, turn, sc in each st across. (10 sc)

Row 12: Ch 1, turn, skip first st, sc in each of next 7 sts, skip next st, sc in last st. (8 sc) Change to Color A.

Row 13: Ch 1, turn, skip first st, sc in each of next 5 sts, skip next st, sc in last st. (6 sc)

Row 14: Ch 1, turn, skip first st, sc in each of next 3 sts, skip next st, sc in last st. (4 sc) Change to Color B.

Rows 15–16: Ch 1, turn, sc in each st across. (4 sc) At the end of Row 16, fasten off and weave in ends.

Apron - before weaving in ends

Apron Edging, Ties and Neck Band

With right side of Apron facing, join Color C with sl st in bottom corner, ch 1, working in sides of rows, sc evenly up to Row 12; *ch 15, sl st in 2nd ch from hook, sl st in each of next 13 ch (apron tie made)*, sc in same st on Row 12, sc evenly up to side of last row, sc in first st on Row 16, ch 14, skip next 2 sts, sl st in last st on Row 16 (neck band made) (Row 16); working in sides of rows, evenly sc to Row 12; repeat from * to * once, sc in same st on Row 12, sc evenly down to bottom corner. Fasten off and weave in all ends.

Creating first apron tie

Creating neck band

Finishing - Use photos as a guide

Position and sew Arms on either side of Body.
Sew Hair Buns to Back of Head.
Sew Head to Body.
Cut out circle of beige felt to fit Face. Embroider tiny stitches for the Eyes and a straight stitch for the Mouth on the felt.

Position the felt Face onto Head and sew in place using back stitches around the edge.
Add blusher to cheeks.

Place Hat on Head and tie on Apron. (Sew them in place, if desired.)
Print out the words "Penny Baker" (or use magazine/newspaper cutting for name) and glue to front of Apron. (Optional - not advised if the doll is for a child.)

Shows position of arm attachment

Hair Buns sewn to each side of Back of Head

Back view of Penny Baker

Dollhouse
BAKERY

The Dollhouse Bakery is certainly a magical place! It's full of delicious tiny dolly treats. Make them all to create your very own Dollhouse Bakery. When Penny Baker moves in with all her bakery treats, your dollhouse will be the happiest dolly home ever.

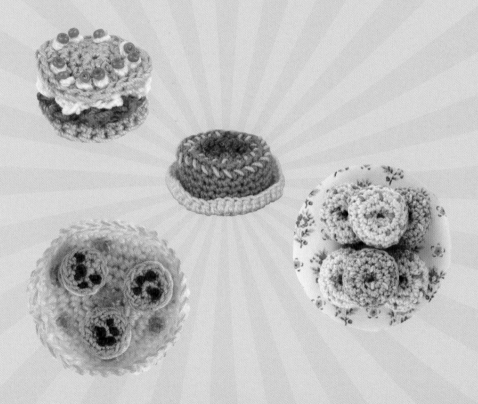

Materials

◎ The finished crochet pieces are all not suitable for young children. The small parts can be swallowed or become a choking hazard.

◎ When using paints, check that they are safe and non-toxic.

For the Projects
Thread (small amounts of each color):
Scheepjes Maxi Sweet Treat 25g

Cherry Gateau
Color A: Topaz (179)
Color B: Old Lace (130)
Color C: Scarlett (192)

◎ Red Seed beads x 10
◎ Glue or sewing thread and needle to attach beads.

Choc Chip Cookies – Plate
Color A: Saffron (249)
Color B: Old Lace (130)
Color C: Black Coffee (162)

◎ Size D-3 (3.25 mm) crochet hook (or suitable size for yarn used) – for Cookie Plate
◎ Green, red and gold acrylic paint and small paint brush – for painted detail on plate. (Optional – or embroider flowers)

Custard Fingers
Color A: Topaz (179)
Color B: Lemonade (403)

◎ Size B-1 (2.25 mm) crochet hook (or suitable size for thread used)

Posh Pink Cake
Color A: Fuschia (786)
Color B: Old Lace (130)
Color C: Scarlett (192)

◎ Embroidery floss or thread in two contrasting colors - for embroidering frosting drizzle.
(Maxi Sweet Treat thread - Lime Juice (392) and Chrystalline (385) – were used in model.)

Ring Donuts
Main Color (MC): Topaz (179)
Color A: Old Rose (408)
Color B: Lemonade (403)
Color C: Chrystalline (385)

◎ Dark pink embroidery floss or thread – for embroidering sprinkles.
(Maxi Sweet Treat thread – Donut Colors A, B & C and Fuschia (786) – were used in model.)

Miniature Wedding Cake
Color A: Old Lace (130)
Color B: Willow (395)
Color C: Antique Mauve (257)

◎ Size B-1 (2.25 mm) crochet hook (or suitable size for thread used)
Pins – for placement of decoration

Scheepjes Catona 50g
Choc Chip Cookies
Color D: Old Lace (130)

Plus – for all projects
◎ Steel # 8 (1.50 mm) crochet hook (or suitable size for thread used) Except for
◎ Custard Fingers and Miniature Wedding Cake.
◎ Yarn needle
◎ Stitch marker/s
◎ Toy stuffing - small amounts

Pattern Notes
◎ Projects are mostly worked in continuous rounds, except for the Custard Fingers which are worked in rows.

Special Stitches

Popcorn Stitch (pc3): Work 3 double crochets in the stitch specified. Remove the hook from the loop. Insert hook in first double crochet made, place loop back on hook and pull through the stitch. Ch 1 to secure.

Popcorn Stitch (pc4): Work 4 double crochets in the stitch specified. Remove the hook from the loop. Insert hook in first double crochet made, place loop back on hook and pull through the stitch. Ch 1 to secure.

Bobble (with 3 dc) (bob): Yarn over, insert hook in stitch or space specified and pull up a loop (3 loops on hook), yarn over, draw through 2 loops on hook (2 loops remain on hook); [yarn over, insert hook in same stitch and pull up a loop, yarn over, draw through 2 loops on hook] twice more (4 loops on hook); yarn over, draw through remaining 4 loops. Ch 1 to secure.

CHERRY GATEAU

Penny Baker keeps a well-organized kitchen when baking.

Base – Top (make 2)

Rnd 1: (Right Side) Using Color A, make a magic ring, 6 sc into ring. (6 sc) DO NOT JOIN. Mark end of round and move marker each round.

Rnd 2: 2 sc in each st around. (12 sc)

Rnd 3: [2 sc in next st, sc in next st] around. (18 sc)

Rnd 4: [2 sc in next st, sc in each of next 2 sts] around. (24 sc) Sl st in next st, and fasten off leaving long tail for sewing.

Cream Filling

Rnd 1: (Right Side) Using Color B, make a magic ring. 8 sc into ring. (8 sc) DO NOT JOIN.

Rnd 2: Pc4 in each st around. (8 popcorns) Fasten off and weave in all ends.

Strawberry Filling

Rnds 1–2: Using Color C, repeat Rounds 1 to 2 of Cream Filling. Fasten off and weave in all ends.

Shows Base, Top, Cream Filling, and Strawberry Filling.

Finishing - Use photos as a guide

Using Color B, embroider 10 French knots evenly around edge of Top. Sew (or glue) a red Bead on top of each knot.
With right sides of Top and Base on the outside, and the Fillings between them, sew all four layers together and weave in all ends.

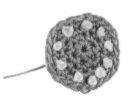

French knots embroidered on Top.

Stitching the four layers together.

Finished Cherry Gateau

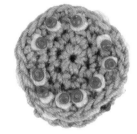

Top view with red seed beads on each French knot.

CHOC CHIP COOKIES

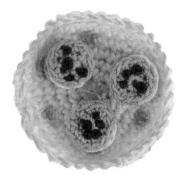

Cookie Halves (make 2 per cookie)

Rnd 1: (Right Side) Using Color A and smaller hook, make a magic ring, 6 sc into ring. (6 sc) DO NOT JOIN. Mark end of round and move marker each round.

Rnd 2: 2 sc in each st around. (12 sc)

Sl st in next st, and fasten off leaving long tail for sewing.

Cream Center (make 1 per cookie)

Rnds 1-2: Using Color B, Rounds 1 to 2 of Cookie Halves.

Sl st in next st, and fasten off leaving long tail for sewing.

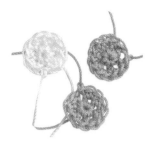

The three cookie layers completed.

Finishing - Use photos as a guide

Using Color C, embroider French Knots randomly on the right side of all Cookie Halves (to create the choc chips).

With right sides of two Cookie Halves on the outside, and a Cream Center between them, sew all three layers together and weave in all ends.

Repeat for all Cookies

Stitching through all three layers.

⊙⊙⊙⊙⊙⊙⊙⊙⊙⊙⊙⊙⊙⊙⊙⊙⊙⊙⊙⊙⊙⊙⊙⊙⊙

Cookie Plate

Rnd 1: (Right Side) Using Color D and larger hook, make a magic ring; 6 sc into ring. (6 sc) DO NOT JOIN. Mark end of round and move marker each round.

Rnd 2: 2 sc in each st around. (12 sc)

Rnd 3: [2 sc in next st, sc in next st] around. (18 sc)

Rnd 4: [2 sc in next st, sc in each of next 2 sts] around. (24 sc)

Rnd 5: [2 sc in next st, sc in each of next 3 sts] around. (30 sc)

Rnd 6: [2 sc in next st, sc in each of next 4 sts] around. (36 sc)

Rnd 7: Working in **back loops** only, sc in each st around. (36 sc)

Fasten off and weave in ends.

Finishing - Use photos as a guide

With right side of Plate facing, apply dots of red paint to create flowers. Make a large flower in the center by painting the 6 sts of Round 1, and make 6 flowers evenly around Round 5. Apply dots of green paint by each flower for leaves. The gold paint is applied to the back loops of the last round – to create a vintage plate effect.

CUSTARD FINGERS

Finger Donuts (make 6)

Row 1: (Right Side) Using Color A, ch 7, sc in 2nd ch from hook, sc in each of next 5 ch. (6 sc)

Rows 2–4: Ch 1, turn, sc in each st across. (6 sc)

Change to Color B.

Row 5: Ch 2, turn, [bob in next st, ch 1, skip next st] twice, bob in last st. (3 bobbles)

Fasten off, leaving a long tail for sewing.

At the end of Row 5.

Finishing - Use photos as a guide

Place a small amount of stuffing onto wrong side and wrap finger donut around stuffing (right side showing). Sew side and ends to close. Making a few stitches through COlor A down the length of the finger helps emphasize the custard

topping (Color B). Weave in all ends.

Placing stuffing on wrong side of Finger Donut.

Wrapping Finger Donut around stuffing

Custard Finger sewn closed

POSH PINK CAKE

Main Cake
Using Color A:

Rnd 1: (Right Side) Make a magic ring; 6 sc into ring. (6 sc) DO NOT JOIN. Mark end of round and move marker each round.

Rnd 2: 2 sc in each st around. (12 sc)

Rnd 3: [2 sc in next st, sc in next st] around. (18 sc)

Rnd 4: [2 sc in next st, sc in each of next 2 sts] around. (24 sc)

Rnd 5: Working in **back loops** only, sc in each st around. (24 sc)

Rnds 6–8: Sc in each st around. (24 sc)

At the end of Round 8, fasten off, leaving a long tail for sewing.

Stuff Cake.

Cake Board
Using Color B:

Rnds 1–4: Repeat Rounds 1 to 4 of Main Cake.

Rnd 5: [2 sc in next st, sc in each of next 3 sts] around. (30 sc)

Rnd 6: [2 sc in next st, sc in each of next 4 sts] around. (36 sc)

Rnd 7: [2 sc in next st, sc in each of next 5 sts] around. (42 sc)

Rnd 8: [2 sc in next st, sc in each of next 6 sts] around. (48 sc)

Fasten off and weave in ends.

Completed Cake Board and stuffed Main Cake

Ready to sew pieces together

Finishing - Use photos as a guide

With right sides facing, position and sew Main Cake on the Cake Board, adding more stuffing if necessary. Weave in all ends.

Using embroidery floss or thread, embroider frosting drizzle lines around the edges.

Using Color C, embroider French knots in the center on top of Main Cake.

RING DONUTS

Penny the Baker needs to test out the bakes herself from time to time!

Donut Base (make 6)
Using MC:

Rnd 1: (Right Side) Ch 8; join with sl st to first ch to form a ring; 2 sc in same st as joining, sc in next ch, [2 sc in next ch, sc in next ch] 3 times. (12 sc)

Rnd 2: [2 sc in next st, sc in next st] around. (18 sc)

Rnd 3: Sc in each st around. (18 sc)

Sl st in next st, and fasten off leaving long tail for sewing.

Donut Top (make 6 – 2 in each Color)

Rnds 1–4: Using Color A, B or C, repeat Rounds 1 to 3 of Donut Base.

Sl st in next st, and fasten off leaving long tail for sewing.

A Base and a Top to make one Donut.

Finishing - Use photos as a guide

With wrong sides together (right sides on the outside), sew the center chains of a Base and a Top together. Wrap a small amount of stuffing around the attached piece, then sew the outer edge of the Base and Top together.
Using the dark pink and thread colors from other donuts, embroider small, straight stitches to the Donut Tops as sprinkles
Weave in all ends.

Center chains sewn together, with stuffing wrapped around.

Sewing the outer edge of Base and Top together.

Finished Ring Donuts with embroidered sprinkles.

MINIATURE WEDDING CAKE

Cake Base

Rnd 1: (Right Side) Using Color A, make a magic ring; 6 sc into ring. (6 sc) DO NOT JOIN. Mark end of round and move marker each round.
Rnd 2: 2 sc in each st around. (12 sc)
Rnd 3: [2 sc in next st, sc in next st] around. (18 sc)
Rnd 4: [2 sc in next st, sc in each of next 2 sts] around. (24 sc)
Rnd 5: [2 sc in next st, sc in each of next 3 sts] around. (30 sc)
Rnd 6: [2 sc in next st, sc in each of next 4 sts] around. (36 sc)
Rnd 7: [2 sc in next st, sc in each of next 5 sts] around. (42 sc)
Rnd 8: [2 sc in next st, sc in each of next 6 sts] around. (48 sc)
Rnd 9: Ch 2, [pc3 in next st, ch 2, skip next st] around; join with sl st to first popcorn. (24 popcorns)
Fasten off and weave in all ends.

Completed Cake Base.

Bottom Tier

Rnds 1–5: Repeat Rounds 1 to 5 of Cake Base
At the end of Round 5, there are 30 sc.
Rnd 6: Working in **back loops** only, sc in each st around. (30 sc)
Rnds 7–10: Working through both loops, sc in each st around. (30 sc)
At the end of Round 10, fasten off, leaving a long tail for sewing.

Bottom Edging Round

With right side facing, working in unused front loops of Round 6, join with sl st to any st; ch 1, sc in same st as joining, [ch 1, sc in next st] around; join with sl st to first sc. (30 sc, 30 ch-1)
Fasten off, leaving a long tail for sewing.

Add stuffing to Bottom Tier.

Top Tier

Rnds 1–3: Repeat Rounds 1 to 3 of Cake Base
At the end of Round 3, there are 18 sc.
Rnd 4: Working in **back loops** only, sc in each st around. (18 sc)
Rnds 5–8: Working through both loops, sc in each st around. (18 sc)
At the end of Round 8, fasten off, leaving a long tail for sewing.

Top Edging Round

With right side facing, working in unused front loops of Round 4, join with sl st to any st; ch 1, sc in same st as joining, [ch 1, sc in next st] around; join with sl st to first sc. (18 sc, 18 ch-1)
Fasten off, leaving a long tail for sewing.
Add stuffing to Top Tier.

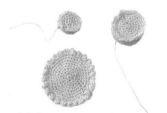

Stuffing added to both tiers.

Completed Cake Base, Top Tier and Bottom Tier.

Frosting for Bottom Tier

Row 1: Using Color A, [ch 8, sl st in 4th ch from hook] 12 times.
Fasten off, leaving a long tail for sewing.

Frosting for Top Tier

Row 1: Using Color A, [ch 6, sl st in 3rd from hook] 12 times.
Fasten off, leaving a long tail for sewing.

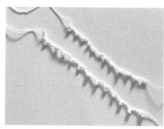

Frosting Strips

Floral Decoration

Row 1: Using Color B, ch 20, sl st in 3rd, [ch 3, sl st in next ch] across.
Fasten off, leaving a long tail for sewing.

Using long tail and yarn needle, bunch up decoration and sew into a round center-piece.

Floral Decoration – before bunching up

Bunched up Floral Decoration

Flowers

Using Color C, embroider about 16 French knots randomly on the Floral Decoration.

Making the French knots

Flowers completed

Finishing - Use photos as a guide

Position and sew Bottom Tier to center of Cake Base, and Top Tier to center of Bottom Tier.

Pin the Frosting Strips around the tiers and sew in place.

Using Color C, embroider French knots amongst the Frosting Strips.

Sew finished Floral Cake Decoration in center of Top Tier.

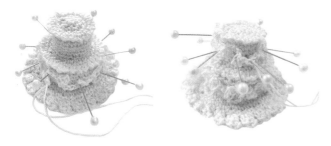

Position Frosting Strips around Tiers using pins.

Cherries

Materials
Yarn
Scheepjes Catona 50g
Color A: Lime (512) - small amount for Cherry Stem
Color B: Rosewood (258) – small amount for Cherries

Plus
⚙ Size D-3 (3.25mm) crochet hook (or suitable size for yarn used)
⚙ Yarn needle
⚙ Stitch marker/s
⚙ Toy stuffing

Cherries
Cherry Stem
Using Color A, ch 11, sc in 2nd ch from hook, sc in each of next 4 ch, 3 sc in next ch, sc in each of last next 4 ch. Fasten off and weave in ends.

Finished Stem before weaving in ends.

Cherry (make 2)
Rnd 1: (Right Side) Using Color B, make a magic ring, 6 sc into ring. (6 sc) DO NOT JOIN. Mark end of round and move marker each round.
Rnd 2: 2 sc in each st around. (12 sc)
Rnd 3: Sc in each st around. (12 sc)
Rnd 4: Sc2tog around. (6 sc)
Fasten off leaving long tail for sewing.

Stuff each Cherry.
Using yarn needle, weave tail through the front loops of stitches on the last round, and pull tight to close.
Sew a Cherry to either end of the Cherry Stem.

Completed Stuffed Cherries before sewing to Stem.

Strawberry

Materials
Yarn
Scheepjes Catona 50g
Color A: Rosewood (258) – small amount for Strawberry
Color B: Lime (512) - small amount for the Strawberry Top

Plus
⚙ Size D-3 (3.25mm) crochet hook (or suitable size for yarn used)
⚙ Yarn needle
⚙ Stitch marker/s
⚙ Toy stuffing

Strawberry
Rnd 1: (Right Side) Using Color A, make magic ring. 6 sc into ring. (6 sc) DO NOT JOIN. Mark end of round and move marker each round.
Rnd 2: Sc in each st around. (6 sc)
Rnd 3: [2 sc in next st, sc in next st] around. (9 sc)
Rnd 4: Sc in each st around. (9 sc)
Rnd 5: [2 sc in next st, sc in each of next 2 sts] around. (12 sc)
Rnds 6–7: Sc in each st around. (12 sc)
- Stuff Strawberry.
Rnd 8: [Sc2tog] around. (6 sc)
Fasten off, leaving a long tail for sewing.

Finish stuffing, if needed.
Using yarn needle, weave tail through the front loops of each of the stitches on the last round, and pull tight to close. Thread yarn through center of Strawberry to form a "dip" and secure. Weave in ends.

Threading yarn through center of Strawberry.

Yarn is pulled through, forming the "dip" at the top.

Strawberry Top

Rnd 1: (Right Side) Using Color B, make a magic ring; [ch 2, sl st in 2nd ch from hook, sc into ring] 5 times, (close magic ring); join with sl st to first ch-st. Fasten off, leaving a tail for sewing.

Sew Strawberry Top onto Strawberry.

Round 1 - prior to closing magic ring.

Magic ring closed with slip stitch.

Completed Strawberry.

Kiwi Fruit Slice

Materials
Yarn
Scheepjes Catona 50g
Color A: English Tea (404) – 1 ball
Color B: Lime (512) – 1 ball

Plus
⚬ Size D-3 (3.25 mm) crochet hook (or suitable size for yarn used)
⚬ Yarn needle
⚬ Stitch marker/s
⚬ Black Embroidery Floss or yarn – for Kiwi Fruit seeds

Kiwi Fruit Slice

Rnd 1: (Right Side) Using Color A, make a magic ring, 6 sc into ring. (6 sc) DO NOT JOIN. Mark end of round and move marker each round.
Rnd 2: 2 sc in each st around. (12sc)
Change to Color B.
Rnd 3: [2 sc in next st, sc in next st] around. (18sc)
Rnd 4: [2 sc in next st, sc in each of next 2 sts] around. (24 sc)
Rnd 5: [2 sc in next st, sc in each of next 3 sts] around. (30 sc)
Row 6: With right side facing, fold flat circle in half (wrong sides together), ch 1, working through both thicknesses, matching stitches, [sl st in next st] across.
Fasten off and weave in all ends.

Using black thread or yarn, embroider French knots for the seeds.

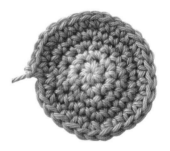

At the end of Round 5, before folding the flat circle.

Completed Kiwi Fruit – With embroidered French knots.

Cupcake Case

Finished Size: About 1⅔" (4.5 cm) hig

Materials
Yarn
Scheepjes Catona 50g
Main Color (MC) – 1 ball

Plus
⚙ Size D-3 (3.25 mm) crochet hook (or suitable size for yarn used)
⚙ Yarn needle
⚙ Stitch marker/s
⚙ Card – small amount to stabilize base

Pattern Notes
The Cupcake Case has a flat base worked in continuous rounds. The sides are textured with post stitches, worked in joined rounds.

Special Stitches
Front Post Double Crochet (FPdc): Yarn over, insert hook from front to back to front around post of specified stitch and pull up a loop (3 loops on hook), [yarn over, draw through 2 loops on hook] twice.

Cupcake Case
Rnd 1: (Right Side) Using MC, make a magic ring, 6 sc into ring. (6 sc) DO NOT JOIN. Mark end of round and move marker each round.
Rnd 2: 2 sc in each st around. (12sc)
Rnd 3: [2 sc in next st, sc in next st] around. (18sc)
Rnd 4: [2 sc in next st, sc in each of next 2 sts] around. (24 sc)
Rnd 5: Sc in each st around. (24 sc)
Work continues in joined rounds.
Rnd 6: Sl st in next st, ch 2 (does NOT count as first dc, now and throughout), dc in each st around; join with sl st to first dc. (24 dc)
Rnd 7: Ch 2, [2 FPdc in next st, FPdc in each of next 3 sts] 6 times; join with sl st to first dc. (30 FPdc)
Rnd 8: Ch 2, [2 FPdc in next st, FPdc in each of next 4 sts] 6 times; join with sl st to first dc. (36 FPdc)
Rnd 9: Ch 2, [2 FPdc in next st, FPdc in each of next 6 sts] 5 times, FPdc in last st; join with sl st to first dc. (41 FPdc)
Rnds 10–11: Ch 2, FPdc in each st around; join with sl st to first dc. (41 FPdc)
At the end of Round 11, fasten off and weave in all ends.

Round 6 – Showing the first few stitches.

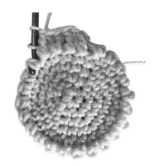

Round 7 – working front post double crochets around.

Finishing – Use photos as a guide
Cut out a circle of card to fit the base of the Cupcake Case. Insert the card circle into the Cupcake Case under the ridge from the first row of post stitches.

Cutting circle of card to fit base.

The card fits under ridge of the first round of post stitches.

Crochet Guide

Crochet seems to have made a trendy come-back in recent times. Crochet is a fun, relaxing pastime that is truly limitless. There are so many inspiring patterns out there to try. Crochet simply uses a hook and yarn to create a fabric. It may look complicated with all that hook wiggling, but it is actually very simple. The stitches, even the complex looking ones, are in fact all derived from the most basic stitches. So, if you learn the few basic stitches you will find you are able to tackle more complex stitches too. If you are new to crochet then here are some basic guidelines to follow. It can be useful to view online "how to crochet" guides or even have a few lessons at your local yarn shop (as I did). And, of course practice makes perfect. It can feel a little daunting to start with, but it won't take you long to fall in love with crochet. All the patterns in this book are suitable for beginners using mainly basic stitches. You may prefer to start making some of the smaller projects first before moving onto the bigger ones. So let's get started.

Following Patterns

Crochet terms and stitches are abbreviated to make the patterns. See a list of abbreviations here and ensure you are familiar with all those included in your chosen pattern prior to starting.

Crochet patterns consist of numbered instructions, in either rows or rounds.

Abbreviations of Basic Stitches

ch	Chain Stitch
sl st	Slip Stitch
sc	Single Crochet Stitch
hdc	Half-Double Crochet Stitch
dc	Double Crochet Stitch
tr	Treble (or Triple) Crochet Stitch

Standard Symbols Used in Patterns

[ ]	Work instructions within brackets as many times as directed
( )	Work instructions within parentheses in same stitch or space indicated
*	Repeat the instructions following the single asterisk as directed
**	1) Repeat instructions between asterisks as many times as directed; or 2) Repeat from a given set of instructions
♥ ♥ ♥	Repeat instructions between hearts as many times as directed

Square brackets and sometimes asterisk (*), are used to avoid unnecessary repetition.

Terminology

All the crochet patterns in this book use American terminology. Please note that English terminology is different so a conversion table can be used here if you are more familiar with English crochet terminology:

US Crochet Terms		UK Crochet Terms	
⬭	Chain	⬭	Chain
●	Slip Stitch	●	Slip Stitch
+	Single Crochet	+	Double Crochet
⊺	Half-Double Crochet	⊺	Half-Treble Crochet
⊤	Double Crochet	⊤	Treble Crochet
⊤	Treble Crochet	⊤	Double Treble Crochet
⊤	Double Treble	⊤	Triple Treble
⬗	Double Crochet Bobble	⬗	Treble Crochet Bobble
◯	Magic Ring	◯	Magic Ring

Crochet Hooks

There are 4 main hook sizes used in the book which are #7 (4.5mm), D-3 (3.25mm), B-1 (2.25mm) and Size 8 (1.50mm).

Please note for the Dollhouse Bakery patterns that use the finer crochet thread, steel crochet hook sizes are given. When in doubt use the metric sizing. US standard size for Steel 1.50mm is 8, 7 or 2! Always use a crochet hook suitable for the yarn/thread you are using.

Crochet Hook Sizes (Rather use this updated table)

Metric	US	UK/Canada
2.00 mm	—	14
2.25 mm	B-1	13
2.50 mm	—	12
2.75 mm	C-2	—
3.00 mm	—	11
3.125 mm	D	—
3.25 mm	D-3	10
3.50 mm	E-4	9
3.75 mm	F-5	—
4.00 mm	G-6	8
4.25 mm	G	—
4.50 mm	#7	7
5.00 mm	H-8	6
5.25 mm	I	—
5.50 mm	I-9	5
6.00 mm	J-10	4
6.50 mm	K-10 ½	3
7.00 mm		2
8.00 mm	L-11	0
9.00 mm	M/N-13	00
10.00 mm	N/P-15	000

There are lots of variety of crochet hooks on the market. I have found the lighter the better. The Clover brand I have found to be the most comfortable to use. You may need to experiment to find your favorite that suits the way you crochet. Ergonomic shaped hooks are also available. Sarah, my crochet friend, loves using these!

Holding the hook

The hook can be held either like a knife or like a pencil in a relaxed way depending on what feels more comfortable.

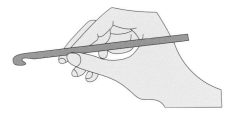

Hold like a pencil

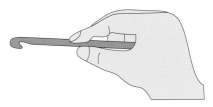

Hold like a knife

The ball end of the yarn can be wrapped around the little finger to create tension during crochet but practice to find what suits you best.

As you crochet take regular breaks to avoid sitting too long or even repetitive strain injuries. Sometimes resting your arm on a cushion can be a useful support if you are doing a lot of crochet.

Gauge (UK term: Tension)

Many patterns you come across will include a gauge (tension) guide.

Gauge has not been included for the patterns in this book because sizing is not crucial. However, it is important to ensure the finished crochet fabric is nice and firm, without any stuffing showing.

Safety Guide

Ensure all parts are sewn very securely.

Be sure to use child-friendly accessories when making toys for young children under 3 and babies. Do not use any beads, buttons or safety eyes due to choking hazards. Instead use embroidery stitches or sew felt pieces for eyes, noses etc.

Some of the patterns in this book include card to add shape, stability and structure to the design. The card can be omitted if the piece is being made for children (or pets), or if you wish to be able to wash the piece.

Some of the Dollhouse Bakery items are very tiny and therefore are only suitable for older children due to the risk of choking for younger children and babies.

Crochet Stitches and Techniques

A step by step guide is included here for each stitch and technique used in this book.
All crochet pieces have a right (correct) side and a wrong (reverse) side. This will be indicated in the pattern.

Slip Knot

Most projects start with a slip knot on the hook. This will not be mentioned in a pattern – it is assumed. To make a slip knot before starting your foundation chain, wrap yarn around hook as shown in the diagram and bring the back yarn under the front one using the hook then pull it tight.

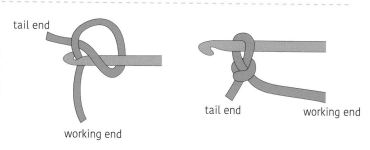

tail end

working end

tail end

working end

Chain Stitch (ch)

With your slip knot on the hook wrap the yarn over the hook and draw this through the loop on the hook.

To make a foundation chain continue to wrap the yarn over the hook again and draw this through the loop on the hook, repeating this as many times as the pattern states.

When counting the number of chains the loop on the hook is not included.

Slip Stitch (sl st)

The slip stitch is commonly used to attach new yarn, to join rounds, or to move to a different position. This stitch does not add any height to your work.

Insert hook into the indicated stitch or space specified and yarn over, draw through the stitch or space and the loop on your hook.

Single Crochet Stitch (sc)

Insert hook in next stitch front to back. Wrap the yarn around the hook and bring it back through to the front of the work; there are now two loops on the hook. To complete the stitch, wrap the yarn around the hook and draw it through both loops.

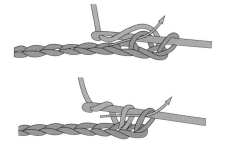

Half Double Crochet Stitch (hdc)

Wrap the yarn over the hook first, then insert hook into the next stitch from front to back. Wrap the yarn around the hook and bring it back through to the front of the work; there are now three loops on the hook. To complete the stitch, wrap the yarn around the hook and draw it through all three loops.

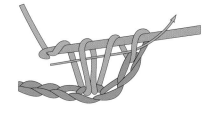

Double Crochet Stitch (dc)

Wrap the yarn over the hook first, then insert hook into the next stitch from front to back. Wrap the yarn around the hook and bring it back through to the front of the work; there are now three loops on the hook. Wrap the yarn around the hook and draw it through the first two loops; there are now two loops on the hook. To complete the stitch, wrap the yarn around the hook and draw it through the remaining two loops.

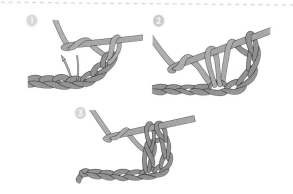

Treble Crochet Stitch (tr)

Yarn over twice before inserting hook in stitch or space specified and draw up a loop (four loops on hook). Yarn over and pull yarn through two loops (three loops remain on hook). Again, yarn over and pull yarn through two loops (two loops remain on hook). Once more yarn over and pull through remaining two loops – first treble made.

 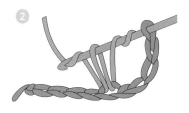  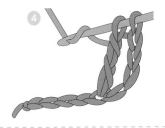

Counting Stitches

It can be a good idea to count the number of stitches at the end of a row or round to check you are correctly sticking to a pattern. Each stitch consists of two loops, one front and one back loop.

Continuous Rounds

Many of the projects in this book use the technique of continuous rounds or seamless rounds. It is a neater way to work in the round. Just place a marker in the last stitch of the round and continue to crochet, to get a seamless fabric.

Increasing

Simply work two of the specified crochet stitches in the same stitch indicated.

Rows or Rounds

Your pattern will either be written in numbered rows or rounds (rnds).

Each row starts by turning the piece and working some chain stitches (turning chain/s). The number of turning chains depends on the height of the stitches used.

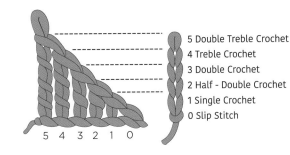

5 Double Treble Crochet
4 Treble Crochet
3 Double Crochet
2 Half - Double Crochet
1 Single Crochet
0 Slip Stitch

5 4 3 2 1 0

Decreasing (sc2tog)

Normal decrease - Insert hook in next stitch and pull up a loop, (two loops on hook). Insert hook in next stitch and pull up a loop (three loops on hook). Yarn over and draw through all three loops on hook – sc2tog made.

Alternatively, if you prefer you could use the invisible method instead:

Invisible decrease - Insert hook into the front loop of each of the next two stitches (3 loops on hook). Yarn over and draw through two loops on the hook (2 loops remain on hook). Yarn over and draw through both loops – sc2tog made.

Popcorn Stitch (pc)

My favorite of the textured stitches! I have used this stitch for quite a few of the patterns in this book as it lends itself to the texture of frosting. It gives lovely raised bobbles by working several stitches into the same stitch and then removing the hook and inserting it in the first stitch and pulling the working loop through. The number of stitches worked in each popcorn varies in some of the patterns in this book, so check before starting work on the pattern.

Make required number of stitches in the same stitch.

Remove hook from the loop. Re-insert hook (front to back) through first stitch of the group and then the last stitch of the group. Place the loop back on hook.

Pull loop through the first stitch. (optional: Make a chain stitch to secure).

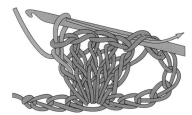 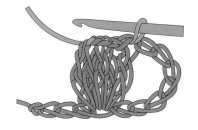

Bobble Stitch (bob)

Bobble stitch is a textured stitch, giving your work a raised surface. Double crochet stitches are worked into the same space. Work your stitches as normal but stop at the final step of drawing yarn through last 2 loops. Keep these loops on your hook and start the next double crochet, into the same stitch but stopping before the final step. Continue working in this way until the required amount of stitches have been made. Yarn over and draw through all loops. Normally a bobble will be secured at the top by a chain stitch. However, not all patterns include this stage so check the pattern.

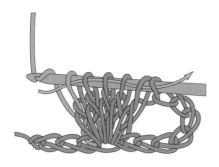 

Surface Slip Stitches

Slip stitches can be worked on the surface of your crochet fabric in the holes created by the stitches to create decoration on the top of the fabric that look like embroidered chain stitches. To start make a slip knot and take it off the hook. Then insert empty hook in the specified place right side to wrong side, place the slip knot on the hook and pull it through leaving the knot on the wrong side of the fabric. Now place hook in next hole and pull up a loop and bring it through the fabric and the loop on the hook – first surface slip stitch made. Continue for as many stitches as specified and then remove hook from last loop, put hook from wrong side to right side in finishing place and pull last loop through and fasten off.

Back Loop Only and Front Loop Only Stitches – sometimes abbreviated to BLO and FLO

Each crochet stitch has a "V" on the top. Unless otherwise specified, all stitches are worked by inserting the hook under both the loops – under the "V". Sometimes a pattern calls for stitches worked in either the front or back loops. These are the two loops that make up the "V". The front loops are the loops closest to you and the back loops are the loops furthest from you. Working in the front or back loops only, creates a decorative ridge (of unworked loops). Sometimes used to create different textures. It is used in this book to create a "fold-line" for pie bases, etc..

Back Loop Only stitches leave Front loops available for use for other stitches to be worked into later, as in the Rose Cupcake design.

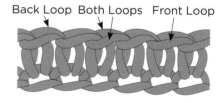

Front Post Double Crochet (FPdc)

This stitch is a textured stitch. I used it for the cupcake cases to give the ribbed effect. The stitch is created by inserting the hook around the "post" of the stitch (from the front side), rather than the front and back loops – see diagram.

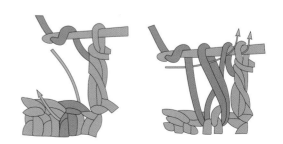

Magic Ring
(also called Magic Circle or Adjustable Ring)

Many patterns start with a magic ring. If you don't want to use a magic ring you can chain 2 and start working into the second chain from the hook instead. I much prefer to use the magic ring technique because it closes the hole completely and it is easy.

Form a loop with the yarn, keeping the tail end of the yarn behind the working yarn.

Insert the hook through the loop (front to back) and pull the working yarn through the loop (back to front). Do not tighten up the loop.

Make a chain stitch to secure the ring. (Never counts as first stitch).

Continue as pattern states with the required number of stitches into the ring. When all stitches are done close the ring by pulling on the tail end. The end can be weaved in after a few rounds are completed.

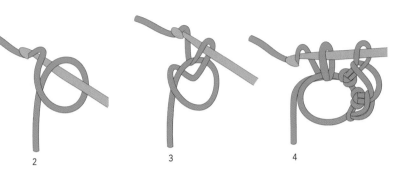

Changing Color

Color changes working in the round and working in rows is exactly the same procedure.

Diagram is shown using single crochet stitches. The same procedure would be used for changing color when working in other stitches, but there may be a different number of loops on the hook.

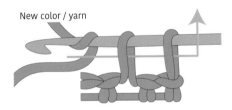

New color / yarn

1. On the last stitch before changing color, do not complete the last part of the stitch. Leave the two loops on the hook. With new color, yarn over.

2. Pull new color through the two loops to complete last stitch.

3. Continue with the new color yarn. The next stitch will be in the new color.

Fasten Off

When instructed in the pattern to fasten off, cut yarn leaving a few inches of yarn (pattern may state to leave a longer tail) and pull the tail through the last loop on the hook to secure.

Stuffing

Use high quality stuffing suitable for children. Breaking up the stuffing before inserting it can help stop unsightly bumps and keeps your project looking more even. How much stuffing is inserted can affect how your project looks so ensure you have enough stuffing inside. If your project has a moving part like a doll arm then you want that part be lightly stuffed so it is easily moveable.

Seams and Joining

In many patterns it advises to fasten off leaving a tail for sewing. This tail can be used to sew seams or join parts. Using needle and yarn, matching stitches and rows where possible. There are various sewing stitches you can use, whipstitch being the most common. Using whipstitch through one stitch loop only helps to blend seams.

Sewing Stuffed Pieces Together

It can help to pin pieces in place first. Use the long tail you left at the end of crocheting to sew stuffed pieces together. Thread end of tail onto yarn needle

Make sure you sew firmly and securely.

Weaving in Ends

Any remaining ends or tails can be weaved into the crochet fabric by inserting the end into a yarn needle and threading it through the bumps on row ends or stitch loops on the foundation chain. For many of the projects in this book which are stuffed projects the yarn needle can be threaded through

the stuffing a few times and trimmed close to the stitches and push the fibres back inside the project.

Thick yarn can be divided into separate strands and woven in different directions to minimise any unsightly bumps.

Embroidery Stitches

A few basic embroidery stitches are used for some of the projects to create detail and interest. It is recommended to embroider through the fibers of the yarn rather than through the "holes" between the stitches.

Back Stitch

Bring threaded needle up from wrong to right side of fabric (1). Insert needle back down a bit before (2) and bring it out a bit ahead (3) on the desired outline. Insert the needle back down through the same hole (1) and bring it out a bit ahead again. Repeat along the desired outline.

Satin Stitch

Bring threaded needle up from wrong to right side of fabric (1). Insert needle along desired outline (2) and bring out close to (1). Insert it back, close to (2) and out close to previous stitch. Repeat making stitches close to each other following the desired shape. Take care to make even stitches that are not too tight so that the fabric still lies flat.

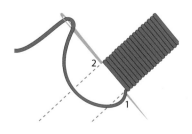

French Knot

Bring threaded needle up from wrong to right side of fabric at the point where you want the knot (1). Wrap the yarn/thread twice around the needle. Insert the needle back through the fabric close to which came up (almost in the same hole as (1). Gently pull the needle and yarn/thread through the wrapped loops to form the knot.

Straight Stitch

Bring threaded needle up from wrong to right side of fabric at the position you want to start the stitch. Insert the needle back into the fabric at the position you want to end the stitch. Repeat for the remaining stitches.